THE OUTBACK GOVERNESS

SARAH WILLIAMS

FREE BOOKS
HATFIELD

Serenade Publishing

Cover design: Lana Pecherczyk.

Top picture courtesy of iStock by Getty Images. River scene by Sarah Williams, Copyright © Sarah Williams

The Outback Governess / Sarah Williams. – 1st ed. AUS English. KDP

ISBN 978-1-973198598

Serenade Publishing

www.serenadepublishing.com

❋ Created with Vellum

Governess Required

Family cattle station near Hughenden seeks an experienced teacher or governess for our 3 grandchildren. The outgoing, energetic children are aged 9, 6 and 4. The six-year-old has mild autism – high functioning but needs extra support and tutelage. Education is delivered via online lessons through Longreach School of the Air. You will need to be energetic, self-motivated and have the ability to remain calm in stressful situations. You will be a role model for the children. Someone who can challenge and inspire as well as encourage their development of a lifelong love of learning. Great wage and conditions for the right person.

CHAPTER ONE

*P*aige had always thought of herself as a country girl.

But this country was different. Mars was supposed to be like this. Hot, dry and uninhabitable. Parched dirt with no signs of life or water. How could anyone live out here?

And the heat! After an hour and a half in a cramped postal van, surrounded by boxes and parcels, with no air conditioning, she was sweltering. The hot sun scalded her skin through the fabric of her sweat-soaked, long-sleeved shirt. How was it possibly this hot?

At nine o'clock in the morning.

In October.

"Here we are then." Jed turned the van into an unmarked driveway and she frowned as the crunch of tyre on gravel battled with the rising noise of the diesel engine. The elderly man had been kind enough to drive her from Hughenden on his postal run. Paige stared through the window, waiting for a house to appear, or an animal. Something, anything. She didn't care what; just some reassuring sign that she hadn't uprooted her life for nothing.

"Currawilla's closest neighbours are the Hendersons." The driver lifted his arm and pointed out the windscreen, bringing with it a whiff of his body odour. Jed had forgotten his deodorant this morning. "They have a govie too. An English sheila named Helen." The old man continued to ramble on, as he had the entire drive, about the local stations in the district. Who lived where and what they were doing. Paige barely listened to a word of it. Her mind racing with anticipation about her new position as governess to three young children.

She was trained and qualified for the role having been a special needs teacher in Ballarat for the last eight years. But from the looks of it, outback Queensland was very different to country Victoria. These flat plains were more like a desert.

A tall solemn windmill spun slowly in the distance with a weathered concrete tank beside it. Finally, a sign of water. Ballarat had been in drought for eight years. She wondered if water was just as precious here, where water was a luxury not to be wasted. Every shower was timed and its runoff was collected in buckets which were then used on the garden or lawn.

She sat up straight as they approached a concrete block building badly in need of a paint. Shade cloth had been strung up to posts around the front to create outdoor shade, since there were no trees in the area.

The engine cut out and Paige scrambled out of the vehicle, eager to stretch and breathe fresh air.

"You'll be right here at Currawilla," Jed said as he pulled her bag from the back of the van and sat it on the gravel beside her. "Hugh and Ruth will take care of you. Lovely people, both of them. Shame what happened to that family. The good die young and all that."

"Thanks, Jed. I appreciate the ride." She watched the mail van drive off, leaving a cloud of bull dust in its wake. Paige extended the handle on her suitcase and rolled it towards the house.

A long phone call last week with Ruth, her new employer, had eased her mind about the remote location but seeing it was something different.

"You'll have your own room and facilities. Even a school house," she had said. "There are lots of govies out here. You'll make lots of friends."

The air held a strange hush as she walked up to the front door. She had expected the three children running around and farmhands working in sheds. But not even the warble of a lonesome magpie broke the eerie silence. She knocked on the wooden door and listened for murmurs from the other side.

Nothing. No response.

Surely Jed dropped me at the right place? He seemed to know all about them so it must be. The house and property looked almost abandoned. She wandered along the side of the house and came across another small building. The door was unlocked so she pulled open the screen and stepped inside. The living room was furnished with a faded blue fabric couch and coffee table. A basic U-shaped kitchen lay behind it. To the left of the living area was a bathroom and a small bedroom. It was simple but adequate for her needs.

At the other end of the building was a bathroom and a work room. Two aging computers sat side by side on a large desk, beside them, some loose paper-work was being weighed down by a set of head phones. This was surely the school room Ruth had mentioned. Paige was grateful for a quiet room away from the disruptions of the main house. She imagined pictures hanging on walls, books in a bookcase and School of the Air being taught over the computer.

Outside a dog started barking and the unmistakable sound of children's voices broke the silence. Paige stepped outside in time to see people walking along a path toward the house.

"Hello!" An older woman called in a merry voice. Paige guessed the short grey hair and weathered face belonged to Ruth. Next to her, a solid looking man wore a dusty Akubra above thick, brown eyebrows and a friendly smile.

The three children raced towards her and circled her.

"Are you Paige?"

"You're pretty."

"Have you seen the schoolroom?"

Paige held up her hands. "One at a time, please."

Ruth clapped her hands and the children fell silent. The older woman extended her hand and Paige shook it. "Sorry we weren't here to meet you. We were down at the shed looking at some newborn kittens."

"They're so cute. You wanna see?" the older girl asked excitedly.

"Maybe later. Paige has just arrived and its smoko time." Their grandfather stepped forward and extended his hand. "I'm Hugh. Nice to meet you."

"This is Layla, she's nine," Ruth introduced the children, "and Brooke here is four."

Brooke grinned at her from a chubby, angelic face framed by dark curly hair. She wore a pink tutu and brown boots. Paige smiled and crouched down at eye level with the small girl. "I love your tutu. Pink is my favourite colour."

She was rewarded with a bright smile. "Mine too. Can you teach me ballet?"

"Maybe." She winked then turned to Layla. "Do you like ballet too?"

Layla's nose wrinkled. "No thanks."

"Where did Scotty go?" Hugh said, looking around.

"He went up to the house already." Layla shrugged and skipped off.

Paige turned to Ruth, and spoke quietly so Brooke wouldn't overhear. "I meant to ask, is Scotty on medication?"

"Yes, and it's really helping to slow him down. He has trouble concentrating and staying on task," Ruth said.

"I understand. So, it's only mild then?"

Ruth nodded. "He has sensory issues too. Loud noises in particular. Even the dogs barking can set him off. He has ear muffs in his room."

"When was he diagnosed?"

"Fiona, his mother, began to notice some things when he was around two. He loved dropping stones into a bucket, he wasn't very social and he didn't talk much."

"I've worked with lots of kids on the spectrum and they tend to be consistently inconsistent." Paige smiled. "But they are just gorgeous kids and I learn as much from them as they learn from me."

Brooke grabbed Paige's hand and started pulling. "Hungry."

As they walked, Ruth asked about her trip. "You must be tired from all that travelling."

Paige had spent all day yesterday travelling–a four-hour flight from Melbourne to Townsville followed by nearly five hours on the bus to Hughenden. Last night she had stayed at the caravan park which was fine, apart from no hot water.

"I am, but I could really use a shower and a change of clothes."

Ruth waved at the building Paige had been exploring. "Let's get you settled in then."

The children's high-pitched chatter could be heard all the way to Paige's room. As she showered and dressed she caught snatches of their animated conversations. Accusations were being tossed around like a stick to a dog. "She stole my doll!", "He hit me!", "Don't copy me!" Typical childish behaviour that steadily grew louder and angrier. Paige pulled on her shoes and left her shoulder-length hair to air dry.

Her heart tightened in her chest. Poor Hugh and Ruth. Nearing retirement age and raising children again. They appeared to be doing a fine job of it, but three children would be hard work for parents in their prime. No wonder they needed a governess.

Her thoughts drifted to her own parents back in Ballarat. They had stopped at two children, blessed with a pigeon pair - a son, and then a daughter two years later. Paige was as close to her brother, Antonio, as she was to her many cousins who were scattered

around country Victoria. Her aunts and uncles had
helped in her upbringing, just as her parents had been
involved in their children's. Theirs was a large
extended family who gathered together for all the holidays. Their Italian background meant ravioli, spaghetti
and minestrone soup were the foundations of the occa-
sions, followed by sweets and trifle. Her mouth
watered remembering.

Hugh was sitting at the dining table reading a newspaper when Paige entered the main house. Ruth's voice
could be heard down the hall, sternly telling the children to be quiet and behave for their new governess.

"Is everything okay?" Paige asked Hugh when he
looked up from the paper.

He sighed heavily. "Just the usual spats. Help yourself to tea. The kettle's boiled."

Paige opened cupboards, familiarising herself
where kitchen essentials were kept. After finding a
mug and spoon she made herself a milky tea and joined
Hugh at the table as Ruth returned. Her face was
flushed.

"Oh good, you made yourself a tea. I certainly need
one after this morning." Ruth reached up to a high shelf
and pulled down a yellow Tupperware container.
"Some biscuits for smoko. Store bought I'm afraid. I
just don't have time to bake anymore."

"Ruth makes some mean ANZAC bikkies." Hugh
smiled as he opened the lid and retrieved two choco-
late chip biscuits.

"Yum." Paige sipped her tea. "Hopefully you'll have more time on your hands now I'm here."

"There are plenty of books and stationary out in the school room. If you need anything else make a list and we can send for it." Ruth placed a mug in front of Hugh and sat next to him with her own.

"That's great, thanks. I brought a lot of things with me too. Especially for Scotty. How is he going?"

Ruth leaned back in her chair. "He needs a lot of one on one attention and he might take a while to warm to you. Let him know you're here to stay. He likes stability. It's hard for him with his father coming and going. He just gets used to Logan being home and then he's off again."

Paige frowned. She didn't know much about their father. "Why is that?"

"Our son works at the mine in Mt Isa. One week on, one week off. He'll be back in a few days."

Hugh sniffed. "They all lived in Mt Isa before Fiona got sick. It all happened so quickly."

"She was diagnosed too late." Ruth's voice was soft and filled with emotion. "She died a month after being diagnosed. Christmas hasn't been the same since."

Paige nodded. "I'll do what I can. Will their father be home for Christmas?"

"Not if he can help it." Hugh snorted. "I don't think he would come back at all if he had his way."

"Now Hugh, that's not true." Ruth placed her hand on her husband's. "Logan just doesn't know how to act around them anymore. Fiona did everything for the kids. He barely knows his own children. I've tried to talk to him about it. He just doesn't want to listen to me."

"That's good for me to know. Maybe I can help them find common interests and bring them together somehow. I'll have a think about it." Paige finished her tea. "Well, I might as well go and get to know them a bit better."

"Good luck." Hugh smiled encouragingly.

Paige took a deep breath before heading down the hall to gather the children. This position would be a challenge, but one she knew she was up for.

Paige followed the sound of the children's whispers and giggles, to a large room at the end of the hall. The room was taken up by a set of bunks, a single bed, a bookcase and a dresser. Clothes and toys were scattered over the floor, the walls were decorated with crayon scribbles and there was a strange smell coming from the closet.

The three children lounged on their beds, sheets twisted at their feet. Their attention was firmly on the tablet screens in front of each of them. Scotty was talking to himself as his small finger moved across the screen.

Brooke looked up first, a smile spread across her

face and her eyes lit up. "Will you play with me?"

Paige's heart melted. She was such a beautiful little girl, eager for love and attention.

"I'll tell you what, we can all play a game after we tidy up this room." Paige crouched to the little girl's level. Brooke bounced off the bed and started shoving things in the dresser. Layla and Scotty didn't move.

"You too." Paige took the tablet from Layla's hands. In return, the girl rolled her eyes and crossed her arms over her chest.

Paige turned to Scotty on the top bunk. She took an educated guess that taking the tablet off him would probably be a mistake so she changed tack.

"Hi Scotty. I'm Paige." She peered over the mattress. His glance rested on her.

"Hi," he whispered back but didn't turn to face her.

"Do you want to play a game with us?"

"What game?"

"How about tag?"

He shook his head vigorously.

"Hide and seek?"

"No."

Paige looked around the room for inspiration. There was a stack of board games next to the bed. They were still in their original packaging. "Snakes and Ladders?" she asked hopefully.

Scotty looked up hopefully. "Is that a board game?"

She nodded at him, walked over to the games and

lifted it from the pile. She placed it on the bed for Scotty to see. A smile spread slowly across his face.

"Okay. You help us tidy up and we can play this game together."

Scotty bounded off the bed and started helping to clean up. Paige turned, eyebrows raised questioningly at Layla.

"Oh, alright." She slid off the bed and in no time the room was clean and beds were made.

They set up the game on the floor and for the next hour played several rounds. Paige helped move counters around the board and chatted to the kids about their likes and dislikes. Scotty sat next to her, one hand on her leg the whole time. He tensed up when he had to move backwards and got fidgety when the girls were taking too long with their turns. Paige began to recognise the signs and pre-empt them before they could turn into a tantrum.

The children were very funny and each had a bright, bubbly personality. Her mind spun with possibilities of how to encourage their learning and creativity. Scotty was fond of dinosaurs and told her all about the marine fossils that had been dug up in the area. She made a note to look this up and make a project out of it. As well as ballet, Brooke liked anything girly, including rainbows, unicorns, singing, and Dora the Explorer. At nine, Layla was on the verge of her tween years. She liked sport and motorbikes, but also had a weakness for make-up and boy bands.

Paige smiled with relief. These were good kids with lots of potential. This would be a great experience for all of them. She would help them to learn all sorts of interesting things and was sure she would learn a lot from them and this outback experience that had only just begun.

CHAPTER TWO

*T*he smell of diesel enveloped him. It was ingrained in his clothes and had seeped into his skin. His nails were embedded with black shadows he could not scrub away, no matter how much he tried. Over ten years in this industry would do that to a man.

Logan was used to it now. The smell didn't bother him anymore. It was part of his life when he was working at the mine. When he was at back at the station his fingers would twitch for a spanner or another tool and he would seek out tractors and machinery to fix.

He was an expert at repairing diesel machines. He understood their intricate operating system. There was always a reason why something wasn't working. Machines were so much easier to fix than people. People were complicated. They couldn't have a gear box replaced or an oil change and go out again, good as new.

He turned the last screw and did a final check everything was as it should be before sliding out from under the enormous orange digger. The screeching sound of a welder being used drowned out all the other workshop noises. There were several machines and parts in the workshop. He had become an expert on huge dump trucks and prime movers. The enormous size of some of the machines still surprised him at times.

His workmates were all cleaning up and putting tools away. Their twelve-hour shift was almost over and his stomach rumbled for a feed. Logan stretched his shoulders and back out. He wasn't the eighteen-year-old boy he had been when he started this job over a decade ago. It was still physically demanding and mentally draining, but he loved it.

The shrill ring of the bell sounded and all work noises were replaced by men's chatter.

"Did you finish the digger?" His boss, Jeremy, nodded towards the machine he had been repairing.

Logan nodded as he washed his hands in the filthy old sink. "Yep. It's good to go back out."

"Cheers. Thought that would take at least another day." Jeremy slapped him on the back. "Appreciate your hard work."

Logan followed his mates out of the workshop and, after gathering his bag he boarded the bus back to their accommodation in town. The fly-in fly-out miners were housed in basic, comfortable rooms. Logan made his way to his own small room where he changed out of his blue work pants, and yellow, hi-vis shirt. He showered, shaved and dressed in jeans and a T-shirt.

He knew the men would be heading to the dining room for dinner or hitting the gym first. Instead he walked out into the warm October air and found his old Land cruiser in the car park. Despite the air-conditioning running flat out, the sun-broiled interior seemed to take forever to cool down. He was one of the few workers who drove in instead of flying. On his week off he drove the seven hours back to his family's cattle station near Hughenden in Flinders Shire. That was a long, lonely drive he never looked forward to. He wondered if he could make up an excuse not to go home when this week was over. He could stay in town and enjoy himself rather than endure the noise and chaos that awaited him. His kids were just so loud and demanding. Fortunately, he still had a few more days in Mt Isa, so he headed towards town instead to enjoy himself.

Lights glittered under a dark night sky and the iconic smelter stacks stood sentinel over the small town and the thousands of people who called Mt Isa home. Logan parked the ute in front of his favourite pub and made his way inside. The pokie rooms were bustling with regulars, slipping cards into slots of machines, hoping to jackpot and win some of their money back. Logan didn't gamble. He worked hard for his pay check and had more important things to spend it on than a punt. He found his regular bar stool and waited for Jack, the bartender, to serve him. It was still early. The miners would come in after dinner. Some local men were standing in the bar area enjoying their beers and each other's company. The restaurant side of the establishment would be filling up with families coming in for the 'kids eat free' promotion. He and Fiona had brought the kids in for dinner sometimes. Back when they still lived in Mt Isa.

Jack placed a schooner glass filled with cold, frothy beer on the bar mat in front of Logan. He was here almost every night so Jack knew what he drank without needing to ask.

"How are you, Jack?" Logan asked the older man. Jack was about his father's age and knew everyone in town and in the mines. It paid to keep on his good side if you didn't want rumours started about something you said or did while at the pub. Logan didn't have anything to be ashamed of, but he liked Jack and they always had interesting conversations.

Jack nodded at him. "You still working on that digger?"

Logan drank deeply from his glass, appreciating the bitter, cold liquid as it cooled his throat. "Just finished it this arvo. Good as new now."

From the corner of his eye he saw her. Long, blonde hair caressing her bare shoulders. He swivelled his chair around so Jess could put her arms around him. Her kiss was passionate and full of desire. His need for her flared at the press of her body.

"Miss me?" she asked like a seductress.

"Of course." He stroked her hair and gazed into her dark brown eyes. At twenty-two she still had perfect skin and a body to match. She could easily be a model, but she had been born and raised in 'The Isa' and wasn't interested in big city life.

Logan had met Jess two years ago when she had started working the bar here. Fiona had not long passed away and Jess was especially kind to him. After a year of flirting he had finally asked her out, and expected her to say no. After all, he was ten years older than her and had a lifetime of baggage at home. But she had taken a chance on him and they were still going strong.

Logan knew he was in good shape, physical work would do that to a man. He still had a headful of jet black hair and Jess always told him he was hot. Mt Isa may be a small town but the men still outnumbered the women. She could have had her pick of eligible, attractive men, not to mention well-off. The long hours and remote location was compensated by a six figure or more a year salary. It was the biggest motivation for workers here, especially with all the health risks associated with mining.

Mt Isa was Logan's second home. It had been since he had finished school and moved out to do his apprenticeship. Until two years ago he had lived in town permanently. But that had all changed after Fiona had gotten sick.

Logan looked around him. The pub was filling up and the noise of boisterous men was increasing.

"Do you want the usual?" Jess leaned in close and whispered in his ear. It caused the familiar need to rise in him.

He kissed her hungrily in response. "Can I have you for dessert?"

A wide smile crossed her smooth, youthful face. "Of course. Better save room."

She flitted away to put in his dinner order and Logan turned his attention back to his beer. After a long slug, he retrieved his mobile from his jeans pocket. There were three missed calls. Shit, he'd forgotten to call home. He looked at the clock on the mobile screen. It was past eight p.m. Layla would still be up but she might be busy with his parents. No, he would call tomorrow and speak to them all.

Guilt trickled down his spine. He would make it up to them on Saturday when he got back to the station. Maybe he'd take the kids fishing or something and give his parents a break.

Fiona had been the love of his life. They had met and married early in life and been happy for many years. She was a wonderful mother, completely devoted to their three children. When Logan had returned home from work he had seen them at their best. Fed, clean and ready for bed. After cuddles and a story, they were asleep. Then he would leave for work before they woke up. Now, Fiona was gone and his kids lived with his parents. For one week Logan would be home and witness every tantrum and argument his children had, and the constant struggles and exhaustion parenthood had to offer. It didn't take long for him to be eager for the long drive back to Mt Isa for another week of long hours, hard work, but, blissfully, no children with their demands and grubby fingers, and faces so like their mother's. He understood why some people would think he was a bad father. But without his salary, they would have nowhere to live.

The Flinders Shire was in drought and Currawilla would have gone under by now had Logan not been putting his wage back into it. These were hard, trying times and the global financial crisis, on top of the long dry years weren't making lives easy in the outback. Not that life on the land was ever easy.

Jess had started dropping hints about coming home with him sometime soon. He didn't want to blend his two worlds. Not yet. Their relationship wasn't serious enough yet. Even though she had often told him how much she adored children, he didn't think she could handle his three. No, things were fine the way they were right now.

Nothing needed to change.

∾

"Anyone here?" Logan called into the seemingly empty house a few days later. He glanced at his watch. It was early afternoon; his mother and the kids should be working on their school work. His father would probably be in the shed or somewhere else on the station.

He headed to his bedroom and dumped his duffel bag on his queen-sized bed. The floral doona cover reminded him of Fiona and a stab of pain jabbed through his heart. He missed her witty sense of humour and gentle warmth. This doona cover was bright and cheerful in contrast to the heart-wrenching sadness he felt when he thought of her.

He shut the door on his memories and the knowledge he'd had a perfect life for a sweet but very brief time.

He inspected the other rooms. To his surprise his children's room was immaculately clean and tidy. The beds were neatly made, the walls were free of crayon drawings, even the mirror above the dresser was sparkling. It was the first time in years that he could see the carpeted floor, free of his children's toys and clothes.

Venturing outside, he walked around the house. There was a freshly planted vegetable patch by the Hills Hoist clothes line. His mother had let her veggie patch go when the children had moved in, she must have decided to start it back up. Good on her, he thought with a smile, wondering if the kids had been allowed to help.

A slight breeze blew hot air over his face and brought with it the sound of children's laughter. He looked toward the trees in the distance. There was a dam there where the kids like to swim.

He wandered in that direction, sweat pooling on his brow from the dry heat. Through the trees he spotted Layla as she did a cannonball into the water. Brooke clapped enthusiastically at her sister's effort.

He stood behind the trees for a moment watching them. He didn't have a clear view through the bush but the strong smell of eucalyptus reminded him of his own childhood summers spent at the same waterhole splashing around with his friends. Those had been so carefree and happy. Before responsibility and obligations took over his life.

Scotty gingerly stepped into the water and started dog paddling into the middle. He didn't usually like water. The noise and sensation would often overwhelm him. Today he seemed happy and relaxed. A pair of arms came around his son's middle. Logan frowned and leaned closer to see who is was.

The slender pale arms were not those of either of his parents. The woman who held Scotty was in waist-high water facing away from him. Wet, dark hair covered her shoulders. Who was this stranger swimming with his kids? His parents hadn't told him they were expecting anyone.

He moved out of the bushes, dry twigs crunching under his heavy footsteps. "Afternoon."

The stranger turned and gazed at him with wide hazel eyes and delicate features. His breath caught for a moment as he was struck by her simple, natural beauty.

"Logan." His mother's voice had him turning in her direction.

"Mum." He frowned as his gaze shifted between the two women.

Layla and Brooke splashed excitedly upon seeing him.

"Dad, watch this." Layla executed a perfect forward roll under water and came back up with a hopeful grin.

"Good job," he called to his daughter. Had she grown in the last week?

Ruth walked over to him and touched his elbow. "Come over here."

"Who is that woman?" His voice was quiet with just a hint of annoyance.

"Her name is Paige. She's a special needs teacher from Victoria."

"What—"

"If you answered your phone, you would know that we hired her to help with the kids. They're way behind in their schoolwork and your father and I just can't manage everything on our own." Ruth was using her don't-mess-with-me voice. Logan knew it well and was surprised it still sent chills up his spine. Like he was a young boy once again being told off for not tidying his room.

"When did she get here?"

"A couple of days ago. She's already made a huge difference. Don't you dare do anything to annoy her. We need her."

"You should have told me you were struggling. I would have helped."

"We did tell you."

Logan pushed his hands deep into his pockets. "How much is she costing?"

If he was honest with himself he had known his parents were struggling. They always seemed so tired and on edge. He realised that, unlike himself, they didn't get a break from the kids. When he returned to the mine they continued to care for and raise his children. Full time, nonstop. It was no wonder they had called in a governess.

"She's worth every cent. You be nice to her." His mother wagged a finger at him, silencing any further argument.

They walked back to the dam. "Paige, this is Logan." Ruth called out.

"Hi. It's nice to meet you." She waved to him as Brooke tried to climb on her back.

He nodded and sent her a tight smile before sitting on the towel next to his mum and watching the children show off for him.

He studied the new addition to the household. She was young and pale. That wouldn't last long. The North Queensland sun was unforgiving. Her skin would brown deeply despite sunscreen and wide brim hats. Snippets of her conversation with the children floated over. Her voice had a lyrical quality to it which made him wonder if she had taken singing lessons at some point.

"I'm hungry," Scotty announced before turning and swimming back to shore.

Paige looked at the other kids who declared they were also starving.

"Okay. Let's go." Paige walked slowly out of the water and Logan watched as inch by inch her body was revealed. Her conservative blue bikini covered only a small portion of her skin. Droplets of water trailed over her bare midriff and legs.

He watched appreciatively as she climbed out of the lake and wrapped herself in a towel. Logan bit his tongue. Jess had an amazing body. Tight, toned and curvy. Paige was small-chested and straight. But it worked on her, adding to the school teacher persona stereotype he was forming of her.

Ruth ran after the kids who already had a head start back to the house. Paige and Logan picked up the remaining towels and walked back to the house together.

"So, you're a governess?"

"I'm a teacher. This is my first time doing the govie thing." She waved her free hand out at the countryside.

He nodded. Fiona had never needed a governess. They had lived in town and had sent the kids to school in Mt Isa. She had always made all the arrangements for day-care and babysitters.

"I guess we'll all figure this out together then."

They made small talk about the weather on the short walk back. Logan felt awkward in her company, and vaguely like he was betraying Jess by being alone with another woman. Not that Jess had anything to worry about. He doubted he and Paige had anything in common except the kids and the station.

His mobile buzzed in his pocket and he pulled it out. Jess's beautiful face appeared on the screen.

"Excuse me," he murmured, turned and walked away a short distance while Paige continued to the house alone.

"Hi, beautiful. I was just thinking about you." From the corner of his eye he watched Paige sweep her hair over one shoulder and wring the water from it. Droplets fell onto the parched earth below. He ignored the feeling that had slammed into his chest.

"Logan? Did you hear me?" Jess's voice held a tone of impatience.

"Sorry. I'm here. What did you say?" He tried to concentrate as Jess rattled off news from her day, but his thoughts remained with the new govie.

Having her here might just be what his family needed.

CHAPTER THREE

*L*ogan was exactly what Paige had expected. Standoffish and abrupt. She had imagined him older. Maybe balding and overweight would have helped make him more likable. But from what she had seen he was not bald or overweight. In fact, he cut quite a figure in his blue jeans and T-shirt. His chin and cheeks were stubble-darkened as though it had been a few days between shaves. She also thought she had seen a small dimple in his chin, but couldn't be sure under the whiskers.

She judged his age to be only a few years older than her - early thirties. With a nine-year-old child that meant he had married young. She wondered what the appeal of settling down so early had been.

After high school Paige had taken a gap year to decide what she wanted to study. She had been attracted to nursing but after spending time teaching English to kids in India she had found her true calling. The switch to special needs education had come after a particularly challenging class. One of her students, Angela had Down Syndrome and needed a lot of extra attention. She had already been kept down two grades and was an easy target for the school bullies. Paige had finally won the battle for funding and a special needs assistant had been employed to sit with Angela and help her with her work. Paige had watched and learned as the assistant, Penny, coaxed the potential out of the young girl. By the end of the year she was reading at a higher level than anyone else in the class. Penny and Paige had formed a close friendship and still kept in touch.

Paige wondered if she would be able to impact Scotty's learning in the same way Penny had enhanced little Angela's. He was a sweet, cautious child, bubbling with potential. She needed to help him harness it and focus on one task at a time.

All the children were eager to learn but bored easily. With two years of sporadic learning and lots of interesting distractions happening around them she could hardly blame them for preferring station work over history lessons.

After changing back into her shorts and a T-shirt she returned to the main house for lunch. With more time on her hands, Ruth had stocked up the pantry with biscuits, cakes, quiches and scrolls. Today a bacon and egg pie was cooling on the dining table. The aroma of pastry and herbs tantalized Paige's tastebuds as she sat down.

The children were soon at her side, eagerly discussing the story she had read them that morning. Logan walked in and seemed to stiffen when he saw her.

Beside the pie, Ruth placed a bowl full of salad. Grated carrot, tomatoes and cucumber made it a rainbow display.

"Yum." Scotty looked hungrily at the salad. Paige helped him scoop out a large serving, with extra cucumbers.

"Since when does he eat vegetables?" Logan asked.

Proudly, Paige ruffled Scotty's hair as he shovelled lettuce into his mouth. "We fixed up the veggie patch and planted seedlings. Scotty loved getting his hands dirty."

"There were worms!" His face lit up. "Lots of worms."

Logan raised his dark eyebrows. "I never would have thought of that."

Paige smiled at Logan and there was a moment of shared pride and respect. He really was very attractive. Now that she could see him clearly, without the shading of his hat, she noted the pale grey of his eyes below thick, dark brows. There were laugh lines at the sides of his eyes and she suddenly longed to see him smile.

Ruth cut into the pie and dished out large slices. "What's the plan for this afternoon then?"

Paige looked around the table. "I think we should do some art."

She was rewarded by whoops of excitement. These were country kids who enjoyed working with their hands in the dirt, mud or paint. Today it might even be a combination of all three.

~

By the end of the day, Paige was exhausted. After saying goodnight to the children, she passed the dining room where Logan sat, slowly turning the pages of an Outback magazine. His thick brown forearms bulged with sinewy strength below his rolled-up sleeves. Despite the aching of her body she determined to get to know this man better.

"Tea?" she asked.

He looked up at her, his steel-grey eyes making her heart jump a beat. "Thanks."

A few minutes later, Paige put the two cups on the table and sat heavily in a chair. Logan closed the magazine and pushed it aside. The front cover, Paige noticed, was a picture of an older woman in a Drizabone jacket. She was the embodiment of resilience with work-roughened hands and skin that had seen too much sun and dusty heat. Her shoulders were squared by years of hard work. These were the unsung, unglamorous heroines of the bush. Their lives full of struggle and difficulties. For years they had supported their weary men, raised and taught their children and worked their fingers to the bone outdoors and in. Paige drew strength and encouragement from these hardy bush women.

"Mum said you're from Victoria." His gravelly tone broke into her thoughts.

"Yes, Ballarat."

"So why such a big change?" He leaned toward her.

She paused for a beat wondering if he was genuinely interested. "I lived and worked in the same job for a long time and needed a change. Plus, the winters are just so cold in Victoria. It snows in Ballarat."

"Really?" His thick eyebrows were raised. "Just wait until you swelter through one of our summers. You might think you've come too far north."

She bit her lip. "Have you always lived in Queensland?"

"No. I worked in Western Australia for a while at a mine there. The Northern Territory too."

"Two states I've never been to." She sipped at her tea. "Australia is such a huge country with so many interesting places and people."

"Have you spent much time on farms or stations?"

"Not really. My cousins have a farm near Daylesford so I go there sometimes. My Nona has a veggie garden and pots full of herbs. She also has chickens and a rooster. When I was a little girl I loved collecting the eggs and cuddling the little chicks."

Her face warmed as she realised she must sound very naive. Over the brief time she had been living on the station, she had become increasingly aware of her inexperience in all facets of property life, and she decided to use every opportunity to gather information so she would better fit in.

"What kind of cattle do you have?"

"Brahman. You can tell because they have big floppy ears and a big hump on their back." He explained that the 10,000-acre station was divided into thirty-five paddocks of varying sizes and the country was mostly Mitchell grass. "At least it is when it's not in drought."

They sat in contented silence for a few minutes, drinking their tea and listening to the unusual silence of the house.

"Did you always want to be a teacher?" He eyed her curiously.

She nodded in reply. "I love teaching kids, especially at the primary level. I had some amazing teachers at the little country school I attended and I always wanted to be just like them."

"Why did you go into special needs?"

She told him about her friend Penny and their experience with Angela. She couldn't help but smile as she thought of all the children she had helped. "They're a pleasure to teach because you can really make a difference. Like with Scotty. He's already come a long way so it's not that he couldn't do it, he just needed a bit of help to get there."

Paige realised Logan was staring at her and heat rose on her skin. She looked away.

"Sorry. It's just, you're so passionate about it. For most people work just pays the bills and passes time. But what you do really makes a difference."

Paige looked up at him from lowered lashes. "Thanks."

Outside, the dogs set up a cacophony of barking in the yard. Logan stood and went to the open window and admonished the noisy animals.

Paige glanced at her watch. It was later than she thought. "I should go. Your children are early risers."

They both reached for her empty cup at the same time and their fingers grazed. He pulled his hand back as though her touch had caused an electric shock.

"Sorry. I'll take care of these." His voice was low and quiet.

Paige nodded back. "I'll see you in the morning."

She turned and walked quietly back to her quarters.

With the image of Logan uppermost in her mind she drifted off to sleep at last.

CHAPTER FOUR

The next day flew by for Paige. The children concentrated better in the morning, so after the first on-air session, where the older children participated in in a webinar style lesson, they continued with academic lessons and saved the hands-on activities like art, craft, music and sport for the afternoons. Once a fortnight, School of the Air held an assembly and there were various visiting guests who would speak at these, just as they would at a regular school.

Brooke would happily colour away while Layla worked independently on the computer, headphones on and eyes glued to the screen. She was behind for her age but catching up at a steady rate. Paige was downloading and personalising their lessons and this was helping to hold their attention.

Paige sat next to Scotty and they diligently went

over his handwriting together. It had already become tidier since she had arrived.

On Friday afternoons, School of the Air hosted online teacher sessions for the tutors to discuss the next week's program, ask any questions and discuss any problems they were having. Specialist teachers would often be invited to talk and Paige had been asked to share her experiences with special needs children.

Paige had made good friends with the other governesses and mothers who also home-schooled. They all shared this unique teaching experience and bonded in a way she never had with other mainstream teachers.

She had started up an easy friendship with a govie from a neighbouring station, Helen was from England and had been at her posting since the Easter break.

After today's teacher meeting, Helen had offered to drive Paige into town for a pub dinner to celebrate the end of another week. It would be her first time out in Hughenden and she was keen for a change of scenery and to see some new faces.

Paige dressed in a knee-length, floral summer dress with short sleeves and a brown belt around her waist. She had missed wearing dresses and make up. Jeans and shorts were more appropriate out here.

"Wow. You look beautiful." Brooke jumped up from the couch when she spotted Paige and gently stroked her dress. Everyone else looked up from their relaxed positions watching the news.

She felt rather than saw Logan's examining stare. Biting her lip, she snuck him a gaze.

"Is it too much?"

"Too late now." Hugh said, looking out the window. "Your ride's here."

Sure enough an old sedan rattled over the cattle grid in front of the house and the horn honked.

"I better go. Good night."

"Have a great time." Hugh smiled at her.

"Call me if you need a lift home." Logan said softly.

She smiled back at him. "Thanks."

She jogged to the car and hugged her friend. Finally meeting in person.

"You're taller than I expected." Helen's accent was starkly different from the Aussie drawl Paige was used to and it reminded her that there was a big wide world out there. It was easy to forget everything beyond the station.

The long drive to town seemed to go by quickly as they chatted like old friends and not two people who had only just met face-to-face for the first time.

The pub was brimming with locals and tourists when they arrived. They found a table and ordered the pubs famous chicken Parmigiana.

The meals did not disappoint. They arrived after a short wait, with a large serving of chips and salad.

"So, what's Logan like? Is he seeing anyone?" Helen leaned in close to her friend.

Paige swallowed her last mouthful of crumbed chicken. "He's nice and I have no idea. I think he's still recovering from his wife's death."

"I hear he's really good looking. Is he muscly? I mean he must be working in the mine, right?"

Reminded of his thick, bronzed arms, Paige reached for her beer. The bitter liquid burned her throat as she finished it off.

"Can we buy you ladies the next round?"

Two smooth-faced men, both in western shirts and jeans were standing close. Beer reeked from every pore of their body. They looked young, too young for Helen or herself.

Helen waved them off. "Sorry boys, I'm driving and we have to get up early with the children."

"You look too young to have kids." The other man-boy slurred. "How many do you have?"

It was Paige's turn to shock them. "I have three and she has two."

The men looked at each other and shook their heads. As they turned and walked away one of them said, "They looked young to me."

Paige and Helen burst into a fit of giggles and watched them try their luck at another table.

"Come on, Mama," Paige drawled in her best southern accent. "Let's go home."

~

They had only gotten a few kilometres when there was a loud thump and the car jolted violently. "Shit," Helen muttered as she pulled off the road and turned her hazard lights on.

The girls climbed out of the car and followed the smell of burnt rubber. The front right tyre had completely blown out.

Paige didn't know much about the mechanics of cars. In Victoria she would have called roadside assistance. "What do we do?"

Helen bit her lip. "Change it, I guess."

"I hope you've got a spare."

It took a few minutes to figure out where the spare would be on the little car and open the compartment. Paige's heart sank. It was empty.

"Damn. I was sure I had one." Helen started pacing.

Paige thought of Logan. He had said to call if there were any problems, and it was only ten, so he'd still be up. She got out her mobile and exhaled when she saw she had reception.

"I'll call Logan. He'll come get us."

Helen nodded her agreement and started packing the car up.

"Hello?" Logan answered the phone quickly.

"Hi, it's Paige."

"Are you alright? Do you need a lift?" His voice was urgent. Was he worried?

"Yeah, we're fine, thanks. Just stranded without a spare tyre."

"I had a feeling when I saw that old car. I'll come get you."

Paige described where they were and apologised for the inconvenience.

"Stay there. I'm coming now," he said before hanging up.

Not a single car passed them until Logan pulled up in his Land Cruiser an hour later. Paige shivered as she thought of what might have happened if her mobile hadn't worked. They could have been stranded out here all night.

"Thanks so much," Helen said as she climbed into the back seat and yawned. "I might just have a nap, if you don't mind. I'm so tired."

"No worries," Logan replied as they drove away from the broken-down car. Logan had promised to call the tow truck first thing in the morning.

"How was your night?" He glanced over at Paige.

"Good. The pub was busy tonight."

"Payday for the workers. It's the pub's biggest night."

Paige smiled and told him about the two drunk boys.

"That's probably Phil and Gav." He laughed. "They're notorious flirts, especially with new girls."

"That makes me feel better, then," she teased.

"It's a long drive." He stretched his fingers on the steering wheel. "Talk to me. Tell me about your family."

Happy to be asked about a topic close to her heart, Paige launched into a description of her relationship with her father and the other cherished members of her family. When she'd finished, she felt suddenly self-conscious. He was looking at her, head tilted, his face unreadable as always. She realized he hadn't said a word for quite some time.

"I guess you probably didn't need to know all that," she said apologetically.

"It's keeping me awake. Keep talking." His voice was husky and held a teasing note that sent her blood pressure rocketing.

She let her eyes linger on him in the glow of the radio's blue light. Broad shoulders, muscular thighs, and tight jeans that hugged his trim hips completed the sexy picture. His biceps bulged beneath the tight sleeves of his T-shirt. He turned around and looked a bit sheepish when he caught her staring.

"Sorry." She turned back to the road. "What do you want to know?"

He looked at her and she was drawn into his gaze. "I want to know everything."

CHAPTER FIVE

o your Weet-Bix taste better all mashed up like that?" Paige asked Brooke the next morning. It was Monday and breakfast seemed to be taking even longer than usual. She had noticed that on weekends the kids wasted very little time over breakfast, sometimes skipping it altogether so they could take part in whatever activities were occurring around the property. But on school days, breakfast was always a drawn-out event.

For Paige, the rest of the weekend had been generally peaceful, leaving her some time alone to recover her energy. She had worked diligently to complete her school preparation for the following week and had called home to catch up on the news. Her brother, Antonio, had been visiting their parents so she talked to him about her life on the station and the animals. He was an engineer and was genuinely interested in what Logan did at the mine.

"He's a diesel fitter. That's all I know." Paige laughed when he wanted more details. "Why don't I put him on and you can talk to him about it?"

"I've had enough." Scotty pushed his half-eaten breakfast away and slouched in his chair.

"You have to eat more than that." Ruth pushed the bowl back at him.

"I said I'm full." Voice raised, he pushed back his chair and stomped off to his room.

Ruth looked apologetically at Paige. "I'm afraid it's going to be one of those days."

Paige gathered the bowls and took them to the sink. "Leave it to me. I have an idea."

It took some coercing to get Scotty out of his room, but the enticement to show her his special sandpit had him leading her to one of the old sheds behind the house.

The pungent, musty smell assailed her nostrils as they entered the dark shed. The morning light spilling in from the door lit up barrels of various animal feed and bags of mineral supplements. Scotty led the way to a corner where Tonka earthmoving toys were parked in a neat row. He sat down and started moving them back and forward in a straight line, making 'Brrm! Brrm!' noises as he went.

Paige sat next to him. The repetitive actions were a symptom of autism. It would have been this kind of behaviour that Fiona would have noticed. It didn't make him dumb, or not normal, he just saw the world differently to other people and couldn't always understand it.

"Can I play too?" she asked.

Scotty nodded but didn't look at her.

She pushed another toy from its space and noticed a small hole filled with little, soft feathers. The hole was manmade, or boy-made in this instance.

"Wow, look at this treasure." She moved aside so Scotty could see what she had found.

"It's mine. Don't move it."

"Did you find all of these?"

He nodded. "I have more. Wanna see?"

She grinned. "Absolutely."

She followed as he led her around the house, showing her all the secret spots where he kept his treasures. Stones, feathers, leaves and gumnuts were his favourite things to collect.

"You can't tell anyone." He looked at her solemnly.

She placed her hand over her heart. "I wouldn't dream of it. It's our little secret."

The days were getting longer and warmer. As Paige stepped out of her air conditioned donga that evening, the heat slammed her and she felt the warm trickle of sweat bead along her brow and spine. She closed the door and walked briskly to the main house. Opening the door, she was greeted by the cool relief. She slipped inside, closing the door behind her and made her way into the dining room.

She was surprised to see the family already sitting around the table waiting to dig into the roast beef, potatoes, peas, beans and corn which was spread out in the middle of the table. The aroma swirled deliciously in the air and Paige's mouth watered.

"Sorry I'm late," she murmured, sitting between Scotty and Brooke.

"Not late at all." Ruth passed around the plates. "Did you have a good day?"

Paige nodded and glanced around at the adults. Her eyes resting on Logan's. "Scotty's handwriting has really improved. He's trying so hard."

Logan ruffled his son's hair affectionately. "Good job."

Scotty shrugged in reply. More interested in the peas on his plate, trying to stab them.

Hugh was noticeably quiet tonight. Paige had gotten used to his deep chuckle and quick wit, but he was sitting there unusually quiet, picking non-committedly at his food.

Logan had followed her gaze. He had noticed it too. Obviously, he knew his father better than she did and had also noticed it. "You okay, Dad?"

Hugh looked up at his son blankly. "Hmm? Yeah, fine." Even his voice sounded weak.

It was the grumbling of the car engine that woke Paige up. It cut through the silence of the night, causing the dogs to start barking.

She wiped sleep from her eyes, climbed out of bed and went to the window. Withdrawing the curtain, she saw lights on in the main house and a flurry of activity.

Slipping into her boots she left her room and hurried over. Were the kids okay? Had something happened?

As she was climbing the front stairs Ruth appeared at the door. The usually composed older woman appeared ruffled and unusually dressed in a baggy t-shirt and shorts. Like she had thrown on the first clothes she had found.

"What's going on?" Paige asked

Ruth looked at her with glassy eyes. "Oh Paige, I was just coming to get you! Hugh is sick. Maybe his heart. "

"Oh no." Goose bumps rose on her arms. "Are the Flying Doctors on their way?"

"We're taking him to the airstrip in town now. Logan's with him in the car already." Ruth clutched at her purse and started down the steps. At the bottom, she turned suddenly. "You'll look after the kids, won't you? Hopefully we'll be back soon."

"Of course. Don't worry about us."

A car horn beeped from the shed.

"Go. Good luck. Call us when you have news," Paige urged.

Ruth ran into the dark night and Paige waited on the stairs until she heard the car engine rev and pull away.

She rubbed her arms as tickles of fear ran down them.

Inside she went straight to check on the kids, pausing when she heard the girls chatting quietly.

"Will Granddad be okay? " Brooke's voice was quivering.

"I'm sure he will be. He's a tough old coot," her older sister said. "Besides, the Flying Doctor is already on their way. They'll be able to fix him up in no time."

There was a pause for a moment before Brooke spoke again, her voice quiet and full of emotion. "They didn't save Mummy."

"Mum had cancer. No one could help her." Layla's answer silenced her sister and when Paige glanced in a few minutes later the girls had their eyes closed and looked at peace.

Paige tried to sleep on the couch, but was kept awake by thoughts of hospitals and death; her mind buzzed wondering how she would help the kids through this traumatic time.

Eventually she gave up on sleep and made herself some tea.

She drank in on the front porch as she watched the countryside come out of its dark slumber.

The porch itself was cluttered with boots and jackets and misplaced belongings. Toys were scattered in corners, forgotten by their owners. A thick sheen of dust and dirt covered the wood-planked veranda and furniture that had seen better days.

Paige shuddered to think what her mother would say if she saw this house. As wonderful as the woman was, she could not stand a messy home. "Messy house, messy life," had always been her mantra.

With her mother in mind, Paige started picking up toys and cleaning away the rubbish.

She had found the broom and was almost finished sweeping by the time Scotty came out and found her.

"Good morning, sweetheart." Paige smiled at him. His hair was messed and his face soft from sleep.

"Morning." His voice was gruff. He looked around. "Where's Grandma?"

Paige bent down so she was on her knees in front of him, eye level. "She and your dad took your granddad to the hospital last night."

He frowned. "Why?"

"Granddad wasn't feeling too well so he's there to get better."

"Okay. Will Dad and Grandma come home soon?"

"I hope so, but until then it's just us and your sisters.

Is that okay?" Paige looked into his eyes. As grey as his fathers.

"I'm hungry. Will you make me breakfast?"

Paige stood up and offered him her hand. "I sure will. Let's go see what we can make."

He clutched her hand and they went back into the house.

There were plenty of eggs, so together they made scrambled eggs on toast and bacon. The aroma lured the girls out of bed and they shared the meal around the dining table, all still dressed in their pyjamas.

When Paige's mobile rang, everyone stopped to stare at it. Ruth's name flashed across the screen causing Paige to gulp back fear. What if she was calling with bad news? How would she tell the kids?

"Finish your food." She stood and took the phone. "I'll be back in a minute."

She slipped outside onto the now-clean veranda and answered the call.

"Hello?"

"It's Logan." His voice was husky.

"How's it going? Is Hugh okay?" She knew she was talking fast, but she couldn't help it.

"He's in Intensive Care. He had a heart attack. Apparently, he has high cholesterol and high blood sugar, but we didn't know because he never goes to the doctor." His voice had an air of frustration to it. "The doctors are surprised it took this long for him to have an episode."

"Oh my God. That's terrible." Paige placed a hand over her heart as emotion rolled through her. She had grown fond of Hugh and enjoyed their friendship. "Is there anything they can do?"

He sighed. "They're still running tests at the moment. We're in Mt Isa, but they may fly him to Townsville yet."

"Okay. What can I do?" She needed to be of use in some way.

"Can you keep looking after the kids? Mum won't leave Dad and I need to stay, at least until we find out what's happening."

"Of course. Don't even worry about us," she urged. "Give Ruth and Hugh our love and keep us updated.

"Thanks, Paige."

"Do you want to talk to the kids?"

He paused. "Um, not right now. I better go check on Dad. I don't want to be away too long."

"No worries. I'll tell them what's happening but keep it optimistic."

"That'd be great. Thanks."

After she ended the call, she took some deep breathes to compose herself.

The kids all looked up expectantly when she returned.

"Is Granddad okay?" Layla asked.

Paige sat down at the table and chose her words carefully. "Your granddad had a heart attack."

The girls gasped and Scotty started to cry.

"Is he dead?" the little boy sobbed. He was one of those kids who felt every emotion keenly.

"No, no. He just needs some more tests so the doctors can figure out what to do to make him better." Paige went to Scott and put her arms around him.

"Really?" He turned his damp eyes on her and she nodded in reply.

"Yes. The doctors are doing all they can."

Scotty turned into her embrace and wrapped his arms tightly around her.

"Is Daddy coming home now?" Brooke asked. The pleading in her voice melted Paige's heart.

"Not yet sweetheart. But soon."

For the first time, she was certain she'd come to the right place. At least she could be a source of stability and comfort for the children during this trying time.

CHAPTER SIX

*P*aige and the children got into a good routine over the next few days. They would wake early, have breakfast, feed the animals, do their chores and some classroom work before coming in for a lunch of sandwiches. Then, more classroom time in the afternoon, always making sure their jobs were done and the house was tidy before dinnertime.

Logan and Ruth would call nightly just as Paige was preparing dinner for the children. Hugh was being transferred to Townsville and Ruth was accompanying him. Logan had applied for leave and would return home as soon as Hugh left Mt Isa hospital. Ruth was doting on her husband and they were already discussing dietary and lifestyle changes.

As they waited for Logan to arrive home, Paige and the children made a game of cleaning the house. They mopped the floors and cleaned the windows so that they gleamed like never before. The layer of dust on the windows had been as thick as her finger, so it was surprising when they were clean just how much sunlight actually filtered through making the house bright and sunny where it had been drab and dark. Unable to call a carpet cleaner, she vacuumed several times to remove the ingrained layers of dust and dirt that were continually traipsed in.

Sheets were changed and laundered. Walls were wiped over and bathrooms were scrubbed until they shone. The children were surprisingly cooperative and eager to help with this project she had set them. They would eagerly come to her and ask, "What's next, Paige?"

When they finally heard Logan's vehicle rumbling up the driveway and clattering over the cattle grid the kids quickly finished what they were doing and gathered outside to greet their father.

Paige watched an expression of joy and relief cross Logan's face as he climbed out of the Land Cruiser and looked at his children. Clean clothes and huge smiles on their faces, eager for his love and affection.

"Wow, look at this house." He gestured at the organised rows of shoes and outside toys.

"Wait until you see inside!" Brooke grinned before running into his arms and hugging him.

After lowering her to the ground, Logan briefly hugged his older children in turn then stopped in front of Paige.

"You've been busy."

"The kids helped. It's been fun. Hasn't it, kids?"

They murmured their agreement.

Logan took off his boots and left them neatly at the front door before walking inside. Paige followed them in and busied herself making tea as the children guided their father through the house showing him their hard work.

"I can't believe it's the same house," he said as he accepted his tea a few minutes later.

"It just needed a little bit of attention. Nothing a good clean up couldn't fix." Paige sank onto the dining room chair next to Logan. "How is Hugh doing?"

Logan's shoulders slumped. "He's still tired and weak. I should have noticed. If I'd known his blood pressure was so high never would have left the kids with them so long." He leaned forward on his forearms. Like he held the weight of the world on his shoulders.

"Don't blame yourself." Paige patted his arm gently. "Ruth and Hugh would do anything for you and the kids. They want what's best for them."

His gaze sought hers. "I really need to thank you for the last few days. I know it's not in your job description."

She smiled back at him. "Don't mention it. I can only imagine what you're going through. If it was my Dad I would be devastated."

"Thanks." She watched his gaze lower to where her hand was still on his arm. She was idly brushing his skin with her thumb. She pulled it back and hid her hands under the table.

"I better get some work done. The jobs will have been piling up and I need to make sure they have something to come back to." Logan stood, and then hesitated briefly before turning back to her. "I'm really glad you're here. We all are."

Her eyes stung. "Don't worry. I'm not going anywhere."

Logan stretched back in the chair, his muscles tense and aching. His father always took care of the bookwork so the columns of numbers on the screen in front of him didn't make much sense.

His phone buzzed and he pulled it out of his jeans pocket.

"Hi Jess," He kept his voice bright and carefree.

"Hi Darling." Jess spoke in her usual chirpy tone. "How're your parents?"

He sighed. "They're on their way to Townsville. They'll need to stay there for a few weeks and get Dad's heart under control"

What would happen if he lost his father? He didn't think he could deal with another death in the family. What would happen to the station? Would he have to sell it? He couldn't run it by himself. It was a huge responsibility. Logan squeezed his eyes shut. He couldn't think like that. He had to be positive. He had to be strong for Mum and his kids.

"Try not to worry, darling. He's in good hands. I'm sure he'll be fine." Jess sounded so sure, but how did she know? She had never even met Hugh. "Listen, I've got the weekend off, how about I drive down?"

Logan felt his body tighten. Jess had never asked to visit before, or meet his family. Currawilla was in the middle of nowhere and she liked the convenience of town life with the shops and social life Mt Isa had to offer. He didn't think cattle and kids would interest her and right now that's all he had. The idea that that was why he kept their relationship casual surfaced. She wasn't cut out for this part of his life.

"Things are a bit crazy right now." He kept his voice soft. "I'm not sure how the kids would take it right now."

"Okay, it was just an idea." Her voice lifted. She almost sounded pleased he had turned her down.

"You won't miss me too much?" He idly opened the email program on his father's computer.

"I can always pick up an extra shift. I'm sure I won't be too lonely."

He murmured in agreement his gaze returning to the screen.

"Hey, guess what? Matt and Hannah finally hooked up."

Logan shook his head trying to remember who she was talking about. His life in Mt Isa seemed so distant and irrelevant right now, with so much going on here. She rattled on for a few minutes about how she had known they were going make good couple.

Logan stopped listening and let his mind wander. He thought about the kids. They were awfully quiet. Perhaps Paige had taken them to the schoolroom, or outside somewhere. They all seemed so much more settled than they had been for a long time. Her positive attitude was certainly rubbing off on them. And the house; he couldn't believe how tidy it was. Even his mother had given up with trying to keep things ordered after the kids moved in. She would love to come home to a tidy, clean home like this.

"Logan, did you hear me?" Jess said.

"Sorry, I've got a lot on my mind."

"I've gotta go, someone is trying to call me on the other line." She cut off the call before he could say goodbye and he was left staring at the phone and wondering why she had called in the first place.

He yawned; the past few nights sleeping on a cot in the hospital had left him bone weary. He was looking forward to sleeping in his own bed tonight and not being disturbed by nurses and other patients. A proper meal would be a nice change from the hospital cafeteria food he had been surviving on. He felt like sausages; big, fatty ones cooked over an open flame. The kids would love that too.

As the idea took hold, his tiredness slipped away

and he found himself planning a surprise night off
for Paige.

The sausages sizzled on the makeshift wood fire pit
that Logan had set up next to the river. The fatty sizzle
of meat cooking over an open flame was enticing and
made his mouth water. The children were happily
amusing themselves by collecting sticks to stoke the
fire and using them as pretend swords. He watched as
they giggled and chased each other around the bush.

Logan was aware of Paige sitting close by, watching
him turn the sausages. The hairs on the back of his
neck prickled under her watchful eye. It wasn't uncomfortable, knowing she found him attractive; he rather
liked the attention. He liked looking at her too. She was
softly feminine and so sweet. She wasn't like the
women he encountered in Mt Isa, newly toughened
from their experience in the harsh, male-dominated
environment of the mining town.

"So, how are you liking the outback?" He moved to
sit next to her on a log.

Paige smiled at him. He loved the way her whole
face smiled at him, not just her rounded pink lips. "It's
certainly a change from Ballarat. But I love it."

Logan had seen enough of cities and large towns to
know the difference was the environment and the pace
of life. There was no noisy traffic roaring past and the

air was fresh and pure. The silence was broken only by the bellowing of a beast, the dogs, or more often than not, his children.

As he thought about it, he realised he was a country boy through and through. He couldn't change the way he was, even when he tried. The city stifled him when he had to visit. He even found Mt Isa stifling with the crowded, noisy streets, traffic blaring cars. Not to mention the pollution from the vehicles and mine sites.

He watched as she waved flies away from her face. "The flies and the heat might take a bit of getting used to."

"I should get you one of those hats, with the corks dangling from string." He grinned at her.

"Do those really exist? I thought that was just a joke we played on tourists."

"I'm sure I could make you one if it comes to that. As for the heat, it will only get hotter in summer." He absently threw a stick on the fire. "Be better if we got some rain." He gazed out at the brown, barren landscape.

Scotty came running towards them and threw himself at Paige.

"Hello, how are you?" She wrapped her arms around him and cuddled him close and then gently tickled his tummy. He giggled with glee and Logan grinned.

"Hungry," he said between chuckles. "Hungry! Hungry!"

"Dinner's almost ready." She turned to Logan with a tender gaze.

A burning smell drew his attention back to the fire pit. He had neglected the cooking sausages, so caught up in his thoughts. Quickly, he turned them over with the tongs, but in doing so he put his fingers too close to the open flame.

"Bugger." He withdrew his hand quickly and shook it.

"Are you okay?" Paige was at his side immediately and reached for his injured hand, turning his palm in her own soft hands.

He watched her curiously. She smelled sweet. Like mango and lychees. His favourite tropical fruits.

"It'll be okay." He shrugged, the biting pain was not nearly as bad as some of the injuries he had sustained in the past, but he did enjoy the attention he was receiving.

"Do you have any aloe vera?" She looked up into his eyes and he was struck by just how dazzling a shade of pale amber brown they were, similar to those of a grey kangaroo.

He shook his head. "I think there's some in the kitchen. But it will be fine."

"Nonsense. I'll go get it. In the meantime, put your hand on this." She handed him an ice-cold water bottle from the esky. The coolness against the burn had a pleasant numbing effect.

"Scotty, come with me. We need to get Daddy some

medicine and I need your help finding it." She scooped up the little boy's hand and they trotted off to the house.

Logan touched his hand where moments ago her fingers had been. It tingled from her touch and her hypnotic scent lingered in the still air around him.

~

Paige found the first aid kit in a kitchen cupboard, just where Scotty had led her. She rifled through bandages and tablet packages until she found a tube of aloe vera ointment.

"Just what Daddy needs." She smiled at the young boy whose big eyes gazed up at her. He looked so like his father, but without the rough, life-hardened edges. Would he grow to be a man like his father? Or would he keep his sweet innocence?

Hand-in-hand they walked back down to the river, following the scent of sausages cooking and the sounds of the girls playing.

Paige knew it the moment Logan's eyes found her. Although still a distance away, she sensed him studying her. A shiver ran down her spine and she licked her dry lips.

It had been a long time since she had felt an attraction to a man, and oh, what a man Logan was. As she drew closer, she dared to look in his direction. His eyes were still on her and she felt her skin warm under his intense gaze.

"Scotty, why don't you go get your sisters?" Logan suggested as Paige sat next to him on the log.

"Can we play for a bit longer?" the young boy pleaded.

"Okay. Just a little longer or the sausages will get cold." The heat had dissolved to fatherly love and Paige wondered if she had imagined the desire in his eyes.

"Give me your hand," she said as she unscrewed the lid of the cream. He offered his reddened palm to her and she studied the lines and calluses there. Squirting cream on her own fingers first, she massaged it into his hand. It was warm from the burn and rough. Her mind drifted, wondering how his hands might feel on her soft skin. Her own loud intake of breath startled her back to reality and she realized she had taken much longer than needed and the cream was well and truly rubbed in. His hand was now resting on her thigh, his body close enough that she could smell his manly scent.

Again, she felt him watching her. She slowly raised her head to find him only a breath away. Eyes glazed with wanting.

She gazed at his mouth, surrounded by dark stubble. Lips parted and ready. She moved slowly, closer and closer…

"Paige!" Brooke shouted, breaking the moment.

Paige jumped up from the log and turned in the young girl's direction.

Brooke stood defiantly, hands on hips. "Layla is being bossy. I don't like it."

Embarrassed and shocked by her own behaviour, Paige scrambled for an excuse to get away from Logan.

"Well, it's time to eat anyway." She pushed her hair away from her face, feeling the heat of her skin. "Let's go get the others."

She hurried off into the bush. Away from the man she had almost kissed.

∽

"Bedtime." Paige clapped her hands. Logan watched from his seat at the dining room table as his children slowly clambered from the couch where they had been watching TV. Although they complained that they weren't tired, Logan could see shadows forming under their eyes.

As they left the room to brush their teeth, Logan turned his attention back to the laptop in front of him. He had just finished off the email, ordering more molasses for the cattle, when he heard the water shut off and the children being herded into their beds.

"Logan, come say goodnight," Paige called out. He frowned to himself. When was the last time he had tucked his children in?

Obediently, he walked down the hallway, glancing

at family photos on the walls as he went. His own childhood captured and displayed as well as his children's. And there was Fiona and himself at their wedding.

"Daddy!" Scotty stretched out his arms as he turned into the doorway. His eyes wide and hopeful. Logan sat next to him and embraced his son. Scotty's slight, bony form curled into him, warm and fresh-smelling from his shower.

"Love you, Daddy." His voice was barely above a whisper. Tears stung at Logan's eyes. He squeezed them shut.

"I love you too, mate."

He opened his eyes in time to see Paige peeking around the door. A smile curving her mouth.

Scotty talked him into reading three story books, and then promptly feel asleep halfway through the first one. Logan gently slid out of his son's tight embrace and gazed at his child for a moment. He looked so like his mother. His heart clenched in that way it always did when thinking of Fiona.

Paige had already read to Brooke and Layla, but they too wanted long cuddles and kisses with their father. Had they always been this affectionate? So in need of attention?

He returned to the kitchen to find Paige cleaning the kitchen benches.

"Do you ever stop cleaning?" he asked as he reached around her for a glass.

She startled and bumped into him. Suddenly they were pressed up against each other. He could feel her softness against his chest. Her breathing came hard and fast, as though she had just been running. She glanced up at him with an unreadable expression. He meant to look away but all he could think was, that for the second time that day he had the strongest desire to kiss her and taste those sweet-looking lips.

She stepped back and bumped against the bench. "Are the kids all in bed? I should give you some privacy."

"Okay." Logan combed his hand through his hair. What was he thinking? Paige was an employee and the best damn governess they could hope to have.

"Goodnight." He watched as she retreated from the house. He would have to hide his emotions better. To lock them away in that part of his heart where Fiona lived on. He couldn't risk being hurt again. He didn't think he could survive it.

Besides, he had been lucky enough to love one woman. A man like him didn't deserve happiness twice in his life. And Paige could do better anyway. She was still young and unattached. She could do anything, live anywhere. This is not the life she would choose. No one would want him and this life.

CHAPTER SEVEN

*L*ook at the size of this monster." Scotty picked up a huge, grey yabbie and waved it in Paige's face. She stepped back with a shudder as the crustacean's nippers thrashed out.

"Put it in the bucket, Scotty." Logan warned and threw her an apologetic look.

Paige watched as he helped Brooke pull on a rope and bring up the net from the river in a rush of water, covering their boots.

Brooke stared in awe at the strange looking creatures and poked a stick at them. This caused them to scuttle around and swipe at the weapon.

Logan opened the net and they pulled out their prisoners before transferring them to the waiting bucket.

"There's plenty here for dinner." Logan grinned as he hoisted the full bucket into the ute and helped the children climb onto the tray. They only had a short drive from the river to the house, and, as much as Paige feared for their safety, she knew it wasn't her place to insist on taking a vehicle with seat belts. This is what country kids did.

"How do you cook them?" she asked Logan as they drove.

"Boil them up in a pot. They taste like crayfish and lobster." He glanced at her. "Hope you like seafood."

Her mouth watered. "I love seafood. My mum makes the most amazing marinara."

He frowned. "Never tried that. It's pasta, right?"

"It's a mixture of mussels, clams and prawns in a yummy tomato sauce. You serve it with spaghetti." She swallowed. "It's delicious."

"Sounds good. I don't think the kids have ever had clams and mussels either."

"It's probably hard to get out here." She smiled thinking about her sojourns into the seafood markets in Melbourne to collect fresh fish for family dinners. Now she was really hungry.

Back at the house, Logan took charge of the cooking, but he had four eager assistants on hand to help. The yabbies were boiled in a big pot on the stove until their shells changed colour.

Logan dumped the red and orange tinged yabbies onto newspaper in the middle of the table and showed them how to pull the tails away from the body and peel them.

"Keep the big claws too, the meat's nice and sweet."

Paige took one, it was still hot from the water, but the kids had already pulled apart many, so she decided she'd better get started. Digging her nails into the middle, she began to pull. She couldn't help squinting and gritting her teeth.

"You got it." Logan reached over and showed her how to remove the shell. His musky scent mingled with the faint river smell of the crustaceans.

Her fingers were sore from the little cuts from the shell and the yabbie juices were probably splattered all over her, but she was having fun.

Brooke started singing as she worked, making up a silly song about being a yabbie. "I'm a little yabbie fat and round, here is my nipper, here is my bum."

Scotty started laughing hysterically at the word bum and soon they all joined in, making up lyrics.

"I'm going to taste yummy in Scotty's tummy."

Logan chuckled. Paige gazed at his happy, wistful expression. She liked hearing him laugh like that. He seemed a man who didn't laugh often, so when he did it was full of warmth and meaning.

Logan buttered slices of bread and handed them around the table. He noticed Paige was grinning from ear to ear, she seemed to really be enjoying herself. She had slipped easily into their family, filling the hole that had been vacant for so long.

He filled his sandwich with the warm yabbie meat and bit into it. Unable to help a sigh escape his lips as the buttery sweetness filled his mouth.

Silence fell as everyone munched through their sandwiches.

"Can we have this every night?" Brooke asked, cheeks full of crust.

"You'll eat all the yabbies in the creek if you do that," Logan teased. His little girl pouted in reply and his heart melted. She was growing up into a beautiful child and he realised just how much he had already missed of her innocent childhood.

Tired and with full tummies, the evening routine lacked its usual chaos and the children were happy enough to go to bed with only one story each.

"Daddy read." Brooke sat in her bed, arms crossed over her chest.

He smiled and slipped under the sheets next to her. Within seconds Scotty and Layla had jumped on the bed too and were snuggling in.

"Paige," Scotty yelled out. "Story."

Paige appeared at the door, drying her hands with a tea towel. "Daddy's reading tonight."

"I want you too." He patted the space next to him on the bed.

Logan smiled at her. "Come on, we'll make room."

She sat at the end of the bed and Scotty curled up on her lap.

One story turned into four. Finally, they were allowed off the bed when Brooke started falling asleep.

Layla crawled to her own bed and was kissed good-night, but Scotty insisted on being carried to his room. Logan placed his son's long body into bed and pulled up the sheets.

"Night night, Daddy."

"Goodnight, son. I love you."

Stepping back, he waited by the door as Paige took her turn. She knelt by the bed and stroked his son's head with gentle fingers. Scotty closed his eyes in sheer delight and for Logan it brought back strong memories of Fiona doing the same thing. He felt his throat constrict, his eyes blurring, and he made a quick exit back to the safety of the kitchen.

He pulled out a can of beer and sat in a recliner in the living room. He retrieved the remote and turned off the TV. Letting quiet settle in the cosy room, filled with photos and childhood memories. He closed his eyes and tried to squeeze away memories of Fiona until white spots filled his eyes.

"Are you okay?" Paige's voice was gentle, like a warm caress.

He swiped at his eyes. "I'm fine, thanks."

She stood next to him. "Today was a good day. Having yabbies for dinner was a great idea." She shifted her weight when he didn't reply. "I'll leave you to it then. Goodnight."

"Goodnight, Paige."

She turned back and he thought he saw something glimmer in eyes.

Later, when crickets throbbed in the quiet night and a cow bellowed to its calf somewhere off in the distance, Logan sat on the old wooden bench on the front veranda, idly threading fishing line and sinkers. His children had enjoyed catching yabbies so much he decided fishing in the river would also be a fun way to pass the time and keep their minds off Dad's illness.

He'd found himself enjoying their company and actually laughing. He hadn't done much of that since Fiona had died. He wouldn't have spent today with the children if his father wasn't sick and if Paige wasn't there. She had been a healthy influence on all of them it seemed. The children were eager to learn and happier than he had seen them in years.

He was fascinated with Paige; her family and history intrigued him. She had deep-seated family bonds that stemmed from respect for her parents and their understanding that they had raised her to be a confident, independent woman who had her family's support and understanding. He hadn't realised it was the way he felt about his own parents. They were helping him through this terrible time in his life, but he suddenly realised how much he was taking their love and support for granted.

He needed to teach his own children by example. A strong role model was what they needed.

Paige's intelligence showed through her eyes. For someone so young she had experience and insight beyond her years. She had already taught him so much about his own children and how best to parent them.

He gazed towards the school house. Light escaped under the curtains in her bedroom and his mind drifted, wondering what she was doing. School planning? Reading a book?

The demountable building got terribly hot in summer. He should talk to his parents about installing air conditioning. Once they had money to spend on frivolous things, that was.

"Dad?"

Logan turned from the donga and saw his oldest daughter standing in the doorway. Her long hair tumbled over her shoulder.

"What are you doing up Layla?"

"I had a bad dream. About Mum." She rubbed at her eyes.

Logan put aside his work and beckoned her to him. She fell into his arms, snuggling her head against his neck. He couldn't remember the last time she had been so affectionate. Maybe as a baby.

"Do you want to talk about it?" He stroked her hair. So much like her mother's.

Layla sniffed. "I was talking to her. Just me and her

like we used to, lying on your bed. Then I woke up and she was gone."

Logan felt the familiar ache in his throat.

"I just miss her so much." Her voice cracked as her tears started, wetting his neck. He held her tight and murmured about how he missed her too and that she was watching them from heaven. What else could he say? He knew nothing would ease the pain of losing such a devoted wife and mother like Fiona. She was one of a kind.

"Daddy, do you think you'll ever get married again?" Layla pulled back and looked in his eyes.

She would know if he was lying and he didn't want to be untruthful.

"I don't know sweetheart. Probably not."

"I hope you do." She leaned back against him. "You made Mummy really happy."

Logan felt the sting start in his eyes, but he couldn't fight it. The tears slid silently from his eyes. Visions of the good times resurfacing from the depths of his memory. They had had a good life once and he vowed to be a better father and ensure his children had a happy, safe childhood.

CHAPTER EIGHT

*T*he schoolroom was buzzing with early morning activity. Paige was at her desk marking papers while Scotty took a speech therapy lesson on one computer, Brooke coloured on the floor and Layla was happily listening into her lesson hosted by her School of the Air teacher. Her headphones in place she watched her teacher online from the studio in Longreach.

Up until the Internet had become mainstream, these lessons would have been taught via postal correspondence or, in the earlier days, over the Royal Flying Doctor radio frequency. This is why it was called School of the Air. The history and sheer reach of the program still amazed Paige and she was proud to be involved in such an innovative program.

The door opened with a screech and Paige's heart

pounded when Logan popped his head around. He motioned to the kids and mouthed an apology.

Paige walked over and stood in front of him, not wanting to distract the children from their work.

He stepped away and she took in the sight of him in his work clothes. Blue pants, worn work boots and a bright orange work shirt with a horizontal fluorescent strip. He smelled like grease and fuel and for some reason she liked it.

"Sorry to interrupt." He wiped his hands on his pants. "I just got off the phone with Mum."

Paige felt her body stiffen. "What's happened? Is Hugh okay?"

"He had surgery yesterday, they didn't want to worry us. He's okay now, he's doing much better."

Relief swamped her and she slumped against the door.

"The thing is, they want him to recuperate in Townsville, so he's close to a hospital and can check in every week."

"That makes sense." She nodded. "They want to make sure he's one hundred percent before he comes home."

Logan scratched his stubble rough cheek. "Yeah. I'm going to put in for more annual leave from work. I know the extra hours aren't in your job description."

Paige held up her hand. "I'm happy to help out as much as I can. You don't need to worry about it at all."

He wore a sad expression that instantly tugged at

her heart. It was raw, open and honest. "It's my fault. I should have stayed here and helped out. I put too much stress on him. The station and the kids..."

Paige stepped closer and laid her hand on his arm, expecting him to flinch away. This was a man who had built barriers up around himself.

He didn't pull away though. Instead, he looked up at her. "Thank you, for all you're doing with the kids and my family. I can't believe how different they are with you here."

"They're great kids. I've grown very fond of them." She smiled before looking over her shoulder at them. "Do you want to grab a quick coffee? They'll be fine for a few minutes." She sensed he needed to talk.

Logan looked out at the land, no doubt thinking about all the jobs he still had to do. "That sounds great."

Paige left Layla in charge before setting off to the homestead with Logan. They walked slowly, their eyes on the path in front of them. Paige chose her words carefully. "This must be a very difficult time for you."

He sighed. "It wasn't so long ago that Fiona was sick. I don't think the kids could cope with losing another loved one." He kicked at the dirt. "I don't think I could either."

Paige rubbed his back gently. His tense, strong muscles flexed under her palms. "You must miss her so much."

He nodded and glanced away. "She was such a great mum. She always knew what the kids needed and never got angry with them." He stopped walking as they came to the stairs. "I miss her so much."

Paige stepped forward and put her arms around him. Her heart was breaking. He returned the embrace, nuzzling his face into her neck.

She closed her eyes, consumed by the gut-wrenching feelings that washed over her. It felt so right when his lips suddenly found hers. When she didn't resist, he kissed her harder. She welcomed it. His mouth opened, so warm and soft, despite his hard exterior. She gripped his shirt, holding him closer as the kiss reached mind-blowing intensity. Her body was alive; every cell was on fire and reacting to his touch.

He drew away suddenly, leaving her lips open, slightly bruised and raw, but still wanting more.

"Shit I'm sorry." He shoved his hands deep into his pockets, turned and hurriedly walked off.

She touched her lips, still tingling with desire. Two deep breaths later she turned and returned to the school room where his children awaited her.

Paige took the children outside for some reading the next day. It was early December and the days were growing long and hot. Very hot. Leaning against an old gum tree, Paige sweat trickled down her spine.

Scotty's hot body was draped over her legs, his head resting on his hands as he read aloud from a story book. His reading was excellent. Well advanced for his age, although his comprehension of the words needed some work, so, every now and then she would stop him and ask him what that meant or why the characters were doing something. He had a long way to go, but he was trying so hard.

Layla sat next to her sister, reading to her. The two girls were such sweet kids and so polite now.

Paige closed her eyes and let her mind drift to their father. Logan had avoided being alone with he since the kiss. Hiding away in the office after the kids' bedtime and always having something else to do.

If she was honest, it wasn't his fault; she'd gotten carried away in the moment too and she'd take it all back if it would fix their friendship. But, oh, what a kiss it had been. She'd never been kissed like that by anyone.

It was inappropriate though. Logan was her employer. The father of these three amazing kids. She wasn't sure if it was against any rules. They were both consenting, single, adults after all. She daydreamed about how perfect a situation it could be. She would have an instant family and could help with the workload, and raising the children. Like a mother.

The kelpie work dog, Max, ran up to them, disturbing the peace with his deep barks. Overhead dozens of pink and grey galahs squawked and flew between the gum trees.

The dog was followed by a big brown horse. Logan

was sitting tall in the saddle. Paige gulped at the sight of him dressed in jeans, checked shirt and an Akubra sitting low on his head. Cowboy fantasies flooded her imagination.

Layla and Brooke jumped up and ran over, cuddling and kissing the animal.

"Where did you get him, Dad?" Layla asked.

"He's on loan from the Armstrong's. They can't afford to feed him with this drought still going, so I offered to keep him here."

Paige took Scotty's hand and they approached the animal warily. Paige had read about the positive effect ponies could sometimes have on autistic children and didn't want to ruin the opportunity. She stroked the horse's smooth neck. The smell of horse and dust assailed her nose.

Scotty watched intently then slowly lifted his hand to the horse's nose. It blew gently against his hand and Scotty giggled.

"Can I have a ride, Dad?" Layla asked, bouncing from foot to foot.

"Well, it turns out the Armstrongs had five horses that needed looking after, so I thought if we took one, we might as well take them all."

The girls whooped with joy before sprinting away in the direction of the house where their surprise would surely be waiting. Scotty was still intently tickling the horse's nostrils.

"What's his name?" Paige asked, admiring the thick white strip on its nose.

"Aztec." Logan replied, watching his son with wonder.

"I think Scotty is quite taken with him."

"Aztec used to live at a riding school for disabled kids. He suggested we try Scotty with him."

Paige nodded. "I've read about it. I'll do some more research but I think it's going to help."

Scotty pressed his face against Aztec's cheek and closed his eyes contentedly.

Logan smiled, "I think he's in love."

Paige and Logan looked at each other over Scotty's head. All the tension between them fell away as they focused on the young boy and what was best for him.

Paige rested against the fence watching the girls contentedly circle the yards on their mounts. Scotty was happy feeding Aztec grass he had picked.

"Come on," Logan called to her.

She looked up at him, eyebrows arched. "What?"

He motioned at Milo who was already saddled up. "Mr Armstrong included all the gear and tack in the loan." He winked at her. "You'll fit nicely."

"No, I don't think so." Paige shook her head.

"Come on, Paige. It's loads of fun," Brooke called over.

"It's okay, I'll lead you around." Logan encouraged. "These poor horses haven't been ridden in a while and need the exercise."

She chewed on her lip for a moment before finally climbing over the fence and approaching the horse.

Logan bent over and linked his hands together. "Put your foot in my hands and I'll give you a boost up."

Paige clambered into the saddle as he instructed. His hands were warm against her jeans as he stretched out the stirrups and placed her feet in them.

She took a loud, steadying breath when he had finished. "Okay. Now what?"

Logan showed her how to hold the reins. "Now just hold on." He pulled gently on the lead rope and led Milo around the yard.

Brooke and Layla let out cheers and words of encouragement. Even Scotty was watching her now, with a shy smile across his face.

"Try to relax. He can feel you're nervous."

Paige let out a breath she hadn't realised she was holding, and tried to relax her muscles.

"He can feel a fly on his rump so you can bet he can feel tension in your legs."

She was getting used to the gentle rocking movement now. "How do you know so much about horses?"

He shot her a smile. "I used to compete in the odd rodeo when I was growing up. All my mates did."

She felt her mouth drop open. Then quickly closed

it as a fly buzzed past. "What kind of events did you enter?"

He turned the pony as they neared the fence line. "All sorts, but I enjoyed roping the most."

Paige tried to imagine what roping was. "Like with a lasso?"

"Yeah." He chuckled warmly. "While riding a horse and the cow is running away from you."

"Were you any good?"

"I had my moments. But it was really just for fun."

A vision on Logan sitting atop a horse, one hand holding the reins and the other swinging a rope while the horse was galloping after a cow, stayed with her for the rest of the day. Even during dinner and the usual madness of bathing the kids and supervising as they brushed their teeth.

That night she had a dream of Logan riding along on his horse, all sinewy muscle and manly scent. He expertly threw his lasso and the rope found its object. As the rope slipped over her bare shoulders it tightened, immobilising her arms to her sides. He dismounted and wound in the rope, forcing her to walk towards him. A pleased grin spread across his face and when she was finally close enough he pulled her to him and kissed her expertly, roughly yet with a passion she had never known.

She awoke suddenly to the sound of a barking dog. Her body was warm and tingly despite the fan whirling furiously above her.

Moaning, she rolled over in bed. How could she ever face him again?

The best thing about being awake most of the night was that Paige was able to watch the sunrise. With a steaming cup of tea in her hand, she sat on her narrow little porch and gazed over the paddocks. She could hear the faint bellow of sleepy animals. The air felt fresh and cool against her skin. The school term was already halfway through. Christmas was only a few weeks away. She would go home for the holidays if Ruth and Hugh were back. Home to Victoria's dry summer heat and beaches. Cappuccinos and her mother's cannelloni.

She smiled as she remembered Christmas in the past. Their huge extended family loudly discussing current events as the adults drank Chianti and devoured the array of smoked ham, ravioli and roast chicken.

The children would happily play outside. Together cousins, siblings and friends would build forts in her mother's garden and play fights with sticks. Their parents would join them for football in a competitive, but friendly match.

Paige gazed at the sky streaked with red and gold. How would this family celebrate Christmas? Another year without their beloved mother, and now with

Hugh's health scare, the adults must all be wondering about their own mortality.

The sky lightened and the few remaining stars were extinguished. Paige sipped at the last of her tea. Life was fleeting. Best to enjoy every moment in the time you have.

$\approx$

The horses whinnied a soft equine hello as the children skipped towards them, their boot-clad feet kicking up dust.

"Wait for me at the gate." Logan picked up his pace to catch up with them.

An afternoon ride was their reward for a productive school day with Paige. She had been beaming with pride when she told him just how well behaved they had been and how much work they had gotten through.

The children had tried to convince Paige into coming with them and having another riding lesson. She had quietly refused, explaining she had classes to plan and things to do.

No doubt she wanted some time to herself, she certainly deserved it. The children were demanding and time consuming, he knew that now he was spending so much time with them. He always thought he was the one doing all the hard work out there in the mine, making the big bucks to put into Currawilla and keep it going. But now he had firsthand experience and he knew just how big a job raising a family was. He had a newfound respect for his mother and for Paige who dedicated so much of her time to children who weren't even hers.

Layla and Brooke were stroking the necks of their ponies when he finally reached the fence.

Logan looked around for his son but didn't find him. "Where's Scotty?"

The girls shrugged and panic rose in his throat. He started jogging to the tack room and skidded as his son appeared from around a shed, leading the pony with a rope.

"Aztec wants an apple." Scotty's voice was soft, he had no idea the worry he'd caused.

"Did you get the halter and lead on him by yourself?"

"Yep. Can I give him an apple now?" Scotty put out his hand expectantly.

Logan reached into his pocket and retrieved one of the three apples he had brought with him. Scotty offered it to his pony who munched and crunched his way through it, saliva and apple juice foaming all over Scotty's hand. The little boy laughed at the tickling sensation and Logan smiled at his son.

With the girls' ponies saddled up and happily strolling around the paddock with their eager young riders aboard, Logan turned his attention to his son. "Do you want to try riding Aztec?"

When Scotty turned away from his father and walked off towards the shed Logan sighed. Not today. It had been going so well. Scotty had been stroking his pony and braiding its mane. Now he seemed disinterested.

"Sorry boy. I tried." Logan tickled Aztec's chin, then turned as he heard the jangling of metal.

Scotty was struggling under the weight of a saddle and blanket. Logan rushed forward and helped his son by taking part of the weight, but still letting Scotty carry the bulk of it.

Silently, father and son saddled up the animal and readied him for a ride. Scotty disappeared again and came back wearing a riding helmet. As well as Mr Armstrong's horse gear, there was still plenty left over from earlier days on the station when Logan had owned horses and ridden regularly. Horses weren't used for mustering on the flat plains now. It was more economical to use utes and motorbikes.

With a leg up, Scotty gracefully swung into the saddle and gripped the reins expertly.

"Ready?" Logan asked after adjusting the stirrups.

After a nod and a grin from his son, Logan took the lead rope and led Aztec in slow circles around the paddock. Scotty never stopped smiling and was soon asking his father to go faster. Aztec trotted for brief periods and Scotty chuckled happily as he was bounced around in the saddle.

Brooke and Layla joined them and together the

family walked and chatted for several laps. Logan, trusting the horse with his son, unclipped the rope and let the kids walk freely.

He leaned on the fence letting the memory settle into his soul, knowing he would never forget today. The sound of his happy children's banter, the smell of the freshly trod dirt and the warmth of the sun on his face.

Fiona would be smiling down on this scene, happy he had finally come home.

CHAPTER NINE

*T*he store room was running low. Paige took the last packet of Weetbix and long-life milk from the shelf and noted the empty spaces where tins and packets had sat. They would have to go shopping.

Paige hadn't spent much time looking around the small community of Hughenden. She remembered hearing of a museum there and when she mentioned it to the kids they wriggled excitedly.

"There is a huge dinosaur skeleton there." Scotty explained about the fossils and treasures he had seen on his last visit.

"We haven't been in years," Layla complained. "It would help for my history project too. There's infor-mation about when Hughenden was farmed with sheep. Can you imagine farming sheep instead of cattle?" She shrugged her shoulders and laughed.

"Hey, I'm from Victoria. Sheep farming is big business there." Paige pretended to be offended.

"Can we go? Can we go? Can we go?" Scotty repeated anxiously, tugging on Paige's arm.

"Please?" Brooke looked up at her with wide eyes.

"Let's ask your father. I'm not sure I can handle you lot all on my own."

The next morning, they piled into the family four-wheel-drive and set off for Hughenden. Logan had happily agreed to the day out. The station work was never-ending and he was yearning for a change of scenery.

He looked at his children in the rear vision mirror, they were planning what to see first and making up stories about when dinosaurs roamed the earth. Paige sat next to him in the passenger's seat. He had barely seen her the last few days, and never alone. They had continued to share meals with the children but when the kids were in bed she quickly retreated to her own donga. He couldn't blame her though. She deserved some time off. He only wished he could give her more.

Driving down the main street, Scotty pointed out every dinosaur picture and statue. The most impressive being the fibreglass replica of a Muttaburrasaurus. Similar to a T-rex it stood on hind legs and had stumpy front arms. "He's called Mutt." Scotty explained. "He was found in Muttaburra. That's real close to here."

"By real close he means three hours away," Logan said.

Scotty took Paige's hand as soon as they climbed out of the car. He pulled her towards the entrance. The girls followed eagerly behind.

Inside, Scotty played tour guide and Logan listened to his son while also reading from the information boards. He soon realised his young son was telling them all the correct information, even getting the smallest details right.

Awe and amazement overwhelmed him. He might have some strange habits and people often thought he was strange, but Logan realised how truly special his son was and how lucky they were to have him in their family.

≈

After Layla had collected information and photographs from the historical displays of shearing sheds, clippers and wool bales, and they had all looked at the fossil and bone displays, they walked down the road to a cafe.

They sat in a shaded courtyard and Paige set out colouring books for Brooke and Scotty.

"You came prepared." Logan gestured to his children.

"They'll get restless waiting for their meals. Best to

give them something to do." Paige said as she set the backpack on the ground.

While they waited for their meals, she encouraged conversation between Logan and Layla. After a slow start, she finally started opening up about how she was going in school and what subjects she enjoyed.

"Tell your Dad about the history project." Paige suggested.

"Well, I have to choose a period from the past and explain how life was different." She said. "So, I chose early settlement in Hughenden, when they farmed sheep."

Paige sat back as their conversation broadened to include early farming methods, foods they would have eaten and bush poetry. It was only when the meals were delivered that they stopped discussing the past.

As usual, Scotty slowly picked at his food and avoided anything red. It meant no tomato sauce on his chips, but he seemed happy to compromise and avoid the dreaded colour.

Sugared up with an ice cream dessert the kids were jumping around and chatting quickly as they left the pub.

"Why don't I take them to the playground over there while you get the groceries?" Paige pointed to the fenced in playground with plenty of trees for shade.

Logan rubbed his chin. "It would be easier than shopping with all of them. Thanks."

She smiled knowingly at him and started rounding up the kids.

"Can I come with you? I know all the brands Nana likes." Layla grabbed her father's arm and tugged on it.

"That would be great, kiddo. Thanks." He smiled down at her. Paige saw the pure, innocent love that can only exist between a father and daughter pass between them.

They headed off to the local supermarket and Paige ushered Scotty and Brooke to the playground.

Scotty happily played alone in the sandpit so Paige was free to push Brooke on the swings.

Another woman and child were also playing and soon met up with them on the monkey bars.

"Are these Ruth's grandchildren?" The woman was in her early thirties with dark hair and a friendly face.

"Yes, they are." Paige smiled, knowing all about small town gossip and how quickly news spread. "I'm their govie, Paige."

"I'm Mel. Our kids are in the same school of the air class."

Paige glanced at the little boy playing with Brooke. "Oh yes. Peter."

Heidi nodded and smiled. "You have done such a great job with them. Especially Scotty."

Paige looked at her young charge, still happily digging in the sand. "He is a very bright little boy."

"Do you have another job lined up for next term? Because I would love to talk to you about coming to our house. We only have two kids but my oldest is really struggling."

Surprised, Paige frowned. "I haven't really thought about it."

"Oh, I just presumed with Logan's fiancée moving down from Mt Isa, she would take over their schooling," Mel said.

Paige froze. "Logan's fiancée?"

"Jess. She's Mary Whittaker's cousin's daughter. I heard she was moving in. It will be nice for Ruth to have another set of hands when she and Hugh come back." Mel kept on talking but Paige didn't hear it. Her head was spinning.

Logan had a fiancée?

He hadn't mentioned her at all. Did Ruth and Hugh know? Did the kids? Surely, they would have spoken of her? How had this been kept from her for two months?

He had kissed her. And all this time he had been engaged?

Disappointment and something else bubbled up in her. The kids were getting a stepmother. That was something to be grateful for at least.

She watched as Brooke sat in the sandpit next to her brother and started to dig a hole next to him.

Paige hoped this new stepmother would love the kids as her own and put their needs above her own. They were so amazing and they deserved a happy life. So did their father. And if this woman, Jess, made him happy, then she was happy for him. For all of them.

CHAPTER TEN

*O*ver the next week Logan watched as the clouds began to build. It was the beginning of the wet season, but the region had already endured a five-year drought and forecasters were hesitantly optimistic of rain.

Each day the sky taunted all the thirsty animals and the parched country below. Starting mid-morning, the clouds would start forming and by mid-afternoon the sky would be full of fluffy grey clouds. But no amount of wishing or praying skywards would persuade it to release even a single drop of moisture.

Logan distracted himself from the weather by donning his grease-stained work clothes and throwing himself into even the tedious drought jobs despite the unrelenting heat. His experience with mine work contributed to his skill set back here on the farm, saving his father the cost of a mechanic.

He had just finished oiling up the tractor when he heard the wheels of the ute rattle over the cattle grate at the entrance of the station. The dogs danced around the vehicle, yapping a welcome--or a warning—to the unknown vehicle.

Logan wasn't expecting any deliveries and it was too early for the mail run. He wiped his hands on a rag as he walked toward the car. It was too small and modern for a local but his frown turned to a smile as he watched his mother climb out of the driver's side.

His pace quickened. "What are you doing here?"

Ruth turned and held her arms out to her son. "We had enough of the sea and crowds and the doctor gave the okay to come home."

Logan hugged his mother, relieved to finally have all his family home again.

"Looks like rain." Hugh's deep voice was full of hope as he climbed out of the low car.

Logan let go of his mother and jogged around to help his father.

"I can do it." Hugh held up a stubborn hand. "The rental company didn't have any utes, so we had to make do with this little thing."

"It made the journey." Ruth opened the boot to reveal bags of shopping. "We picked up a few things while we were in Townsville."

"I'm glad you're back. You look better, Dad."

Hugh was looking healthier and refreshed and Logan knew the rest had been sorely needed.

They chatted over farm business as Logan took in the shopping and Ruth made cups of tea.

"How are the kids? Is Paige working out?" Ruth asked as they finally sat down for afternoon smoko.

"They're doing really well. They work until three so they should be over soon." Logan sipped his tea.

"And Paige?" His mother's gaze narrowed on him.

"She's great. The kids love her. Scotty has really come along with his work too."

Ruth and Hugh exchanged a look. Logan was about to ask them what it meant when the door burst open.

"You're home." Brooke flung her arms around her grandfather and Layla hugged her nana. "I missed you."

Scotty stood next to his father and reached for a biscuit on the table.

"I hear you've been too busy to miss us." Hugh smiled fondly at his grandchildren. "Did you really visit my old friend, Mutt, without me?"

Scotty blasted into a descriptive retelling of their visit to the museum as his grandparents listened attentively and the girls chewed on biscuits.

Logan turned to the window where he could see the schoolhouse. Paige must still be tiding up. She was so devoted to her work and the children's education. She had been amazing these past few weeks, helping him with their routines and making meals. They owed her so much. He wondered what he could do for her to show her their appreciation.

"Dad!" Brooke's voice pulled him back to reality. "Can we show them the ponies?"

"Yes, of course." Logan said and finished off the last of his tea. "Just wait until you see these kids on horseback. Regular little cowboys."

"And girls." Brooke and Layla corrected at the same time, and then laughed at themselves. From the corner of his eye he watched his parents exchange a knowing look and the hint of a smile.

Paige watched the kids prance around on their ponies from the safety of her room. They needed family time together to make memories, and she wasn't part of their family.

The creeping realisation that she wished she was, hit her. She loved those kids. She couldn't love them more if they were her own. Hugh and Ruth were wonderful people. And Logan. Well, her feelings for Logan were more complicated.

Perhaps if they had met under different circumstances and he wasn't her boss. She couldn't deny she felt more than just friendship for him. But the circumstances were what they were and he was already in a relationship. She would not interfere with that and risk doing anything to hurt the family. They had already been through enough.

The family settled into a pleasant, happy routine now that everyone was back under the one roof, happy and healthy. Hugh stayed close to the house and let Logan continue running the station. Logan and his father worked well as a team and he was starting to enjoy being on the land again, working with cattle and horses instead of greasy machinery and work-toughened men.

With less than a month until Christmas, Ruth and the children started decorating the house. Obediently, Logan cut a tree and hoisted it into position, ready for decorating.

"I'm so glad you're here this year," Brooke said, kissing her father on the cheek before sitting down to the evening meal.

Paige sent him a questioning look. "Aren't you always with them for the holiday?"

Logan looked intently at his plate.

Ruth turned to her with a sombre expression. "Logan hasn't had a Christmas with us since Fiona... Well, since they moved in."

"Oh." Paige raised her eyebrows.

"Their mother always made a big deal of Christmas," Hugh explained from her other side. "Presents, a big meal and a special plum pudding with coins inside."

The kids looked over at the adults at the mention of pudding.

"Dessert?" Brooke asked hopefully.

"Yes, actually." Ruth started stacking plates. I think we have some jelly and ice-cream for some well-behaved little kids."

The children gathered up the remaining dishes and followed their grandmother to the kitchen.

Hugh turned to Paige, emotion clouding his eyes. "What a transformation since you came. How is their school work coming along?"

Logan smiled at the heartfelt words his father had just given. Hugh rarely gave praise and only when he felt it was truly deserved.

"They're still further behind than I would like. The school term is up next week and they still have a few assessments to catch up on."

"Do they have to finish next week?" Hugh asked, "I mean, you run the classes can you keep going a bit longer?"

Paige thought about it. "I guess I could, except for the on-air lessons. But it's all catch up and revision anyway."

"When are you going home? Is there enough time?" Logan wriggled in his seat. The idea of her leaving at all causing him to panic.

"I promised my family I'd be home by Christmas Eve but I haven't booked by flights yet."

"You are welcome to stay here for Christmas." Ruth said returning with bowls of jelly and vanilla ice-cream.

"I'd love too, but I already promised my family." She smiled apologetically

"What is Christmas like? With your family?" Layla asked.

Paige smiled, her face lighting up as she remembered her loved ones back home. "We have it every year at my Nona's house. That's grandmother in Italian. All the aunts, uncles and cousins come and we eat pasta, antipasto and pastries. My Nona is an amazing cook and we all eat too much and fall asleep, afterwards. Then we go outside and play together."

Layla grinned dreamily. "Sounds fantastic."

Scotty finished his dessert and looked up. "Mum used to read us that book, 'How the Grinch Stole Christmas'."

"I love that book. In fact, I have a copy of it in the school room." Her voice lowered as though she was telling him a secret.

Scotty's back straightened. "Will you read it to us tonight?"

The girls joined in with, "Yes please," and "Would you?"

Paige looked at the adults around the table, her gaze finding Logan's. Silently asking permission to do something sacred between the children and their mother. He nodded and smiled. "Fiona would have loved that."

Bedtime was made easier that night as the children were eager for their story so moved quickly through their bedtime routines. Logan found himself contemplatively sitting on the porch, the dark, starless night laid out in front of him.

The pain he had felt at Fiona's death was becoming a dull throb. His heart was full of love for his children and parents and there was a spot there for Paige too. She was such an important member of the family now, he couldn't imagine her not being there, even for a few weeks over the holidays.

Absently, he pulled his mobile from his pocket and turned it on to see a bunch of missed calls and messages from Jess.

The pretty blonde from Mt Isa didn't belong in this world of dirt and dust. She was part of his other life. The life he thought he'd wanted. But now...

He read her affectionate message. She missed him and wished he would come back.

Would things be the same when he returned to work? Would he still be attracted to her? He couldn't help but compare her to Paige. Paige had the maturity and knowledge of an older woman and compassion Jess lacked.

Jess was self-centred and young. She still believed the world owed her something. Was that the kind of woman he wanted to spend his life with? The role model for his children? The niggling doubt was getting stronger every day.

His father's heavy footsteps had Logan quickly putting his phone back in his pocket before sending a reply.

"That Paige is really something." Hugh sat down next to his son.

Logan murmured in agreement. In the dark, he couldn't see Hugh's face, but he had the feeling there was a deeper meaning in those words.

"The kids really love her. And Scotty, well, he's like a whole new kid."

"She knows what she's doing that's for sure. I mean, she did train as a teacher." Logan stretched his arms above his head.

"It's certainly an advantage for them having a governess and not relying on Ruth and me anymore. It was such a long time since we were in school we don't remember half the stuff."

"Things have certainly changed. But Mum did okay with me when I did School of the Air."

"Yes, but we had station hands back then and we weren't in drought either. She had more time and energy back in the day." Hugh's voice had become quieter and more reflective. "I might be the one recovering from a heart attack, but Ruth hasn't had it easy these last years. She wakes up sore and aching and barely stops moving throughout the day. She's already lived longer than anyone else in her family ever did and she's not even that old."

Logan stared out into the dark night and mulled over what his father was saying. He had put too much on them when he moved the kids back. But now they were happy and settled.

"We'll hire a station hand after Christmas and I'm sure Paige will come back next term." Logan couldn't see any reason why she wouldn't stay on. She fitted in so well and seemed to like it here.

"Paige is important here. Don't do anything to scare her away."

Logan turned at his father's words which seemed to be edged with warning.

CHAPTER ELEVEN

*A*s Christmas drew closer the weather heated up and the clouds continued to threaten rain, but it never fell. The relentless heat was making everyone restless in class, so when they finally completed the last assignment everyone, including Paige, was relieved. To celebrate she took the children to the dam for a swim in the cool water.

Layla and Scotty took turns swinging of the rope attached to a giant overhanging gum branch, while Paige and Brooke splashed around together in the shallower water. The heat of the late afternoon was oppressive and Paige enjoyed the feeling of the water on her skin.

"Hello," Logan's timbre voice called from the edge of the dam and Paige turned to see him dressed only in swim shorts. His muscular, broad chest was covered in dark hair.

Her face burned as she realised she was staring. "Come to join us?"

He started to wade into the water and her eyes were drawn to his narrow waist and the trail of hair that lead down, below his shorts.

She turned her head, hoping he hadn't noticed.

Logan floated on the surface of the water, his eyes closed allowing Paige to study his peaceful face. He really was incredibly attractive. Heat spread throughout her body. She turned her attention back to the children.

"Swim out to me," she called to Brooke as she practised her strokes.

"Watch me, Daddy." Brooke dived into the water a few metres away and started splashing and kicking, turning her head to catch a breath.

Paige watched her and as Brooke got closer, she stepped backwards. As she took a step her back collided with something tall and hard.

Warm hands gently pressed against her upper arms and she spun around in Logan's embrace. His eyes were dark, his mouth open. She inhaled his rich, damp scent.

"Did you see that?" Brooke asked tapping insistently on Logan's on the arm. Paige stepped back, turned and dived into the water. She re-emerged on the other side of the dam. Her heart thudded and she took deep breaths, willing it to slow down.

The children surrounded Logan now, begging for

piggyback rides and cannon balls. She couldn't help but smile at the way they interacted now. The children were no longer wary of their father when he indulged them and showed affection. Happily scooping them up one by one in his arms, kissing their cheeks and tickling their tummies.

Suddenly thunder boomed overhead. Everyone scrambled out of the water as a familiar, pattering noise started.

Away from the sheltering trees, Paige turned her face up to the darkened sky. The raindrops started slowly but increased until it was so loud she could barely hear the whoops and yells from the children.

"Finally!" Logan bellowed "The rain's here!"

Paige turned to him. He was grinning from ear to ear, pure joy shining from his face. Their eyes met. Suddenly he strode over and lifted her into his arms and spun her around.

She closed her eyes, laughing and enjoying the feeling of his wet, half-naked body against hers, the earth spinning around her.

To Logan the start of the rain was a time for celebration and fresh starts. The thirsty earth would start to recover and grass would grow. Just like his relationship with his family had healed, so too would the land.

Cracks in the ground transformed into miniature

river systems that merged. The tangy scent of the rain on the earth swirled around them and for the first time in weeks they felt cool.

The kids skipped ahead as he and Paige walked slowly up to the house, their hands touching every now and then when they got too close.

Ruth met them with towels at the door. "There's someone here to see you," she said under her breath.

Logan took the towel and patted himself down before stepping into the living room.

"Jess." She looked younger than he remembered. Her blonde hair fell across her bare shoulders. She wore a tight white singlet and sparkly denim shorts. To complete the cowgirl outfit, he noted she wore her favourite hot pink boots.

She flung her arms around him. "Surprise," she purred into his ear.

His gaze turned to Paige. Wide-eyed she watched the scene unfurl.

He pushed Jess away from him. "Jess, this is my Mum and Dad, Ruth and Hugh."

Jess nodded at them, "Yes, we've met."

"These," he pointed to his children, "are my children Layla, Brooke and Scotty."

Jess gazed down at the children with a tight smile. "Hi, kids."

They didn't reply, just continued to stare. Scotty was holding onto Paige's arm.

"And this is Paige-"

"The governess." Jess finished the introduction for him. "I've been hearing all about you from Ruth and Hugh."

"Oh," Paige said, glancing at her employers, not sure what to say. "It's nice to meet you. I should get these kids dried off."

"Yes." Ruth waved them out the door. "Have your showers and get ready for dinner."

Logan took Jess's hand. "Can I have a word?"

"You can have more than that." She raised a perfectly arched brow at him as he gently led her out to the porch.

Away from prying eyes, he swept a hand through his wet hair. "What are you doing here?"

"I've come to spend Christmas with you. You'd know that if you answered your phone." She ran her fingers up his chest. "I've missed you." She started running hot kisses over his neck in that seductive way she once had.

He pushed her away gently and held her at arm's length. "Not here. My kids and parents are right there."

The look she gave him told him she did not like being refused.

"Christmas is only a couple of days away and I'll be back in Mt Isa before you know it."

"Well, I'm here now and I want to learn all about the station. You must be thrilled it's raining."

He gazed out at the paddocks, darkened now from

rain. "I am. It's the best thing that could have happened right now."

∽

The frogs that had long been hiding in the few remaining damp places suddenly returned and the throb of their combined voices pierced through the roar of the rain.

Paige made sure she packed every single piece of her belongings. She would not return after the holidays. It was too hard battling with her feelings for Logan and having to watch him with Jess. Dinner last night had been terribly uncomfortable. The children went out of their way to be rude and disrespectful. Qualities she had thought she had trained them out of. Meanwhile Jess flaunted her slim, young body at Logan and sweet talked his parents. Paige couldn't stand it.

Ruth was making small talk as the two women packed up Paige's room. Ruth was carefully folding cloths while Paige chucked things on the bed.

"It's a shame you can't stay for the Henderson's party. All the neighbours come. It's so much fun."

"What's that?" Paige asked distractedly as she packed her toiletries.

"Our neighbours, the Hendersons. Every year they have a wonderful Christmas Eve party with music and dancing."

Paige stilled as she tried to remember where she had put her toothbrush.

The door opened and with it came a gust of wind and rain. The storm had continued all night and was showing no sign of stopping. Hugh stepped in from under an umbrella.

"Sorry, Paige, you're not going anywhere today. They've closed the roads."

"What? Why?" Paige dropped onto the bed.

Hugh pointed out the window. "The rain. Roads are flooded in and out of town."

"What about the airport? I could take a plane."

Hugh shook his head. "Even if a plane could take off it's not safe to fly."

The door opened again. Scotty walked in and straight to Paige, a big grin on his face.

"What are you smiling about?" She sighed and gathered him to her for a comforting hug.

"My Christmas wish came true." He squeezed her tightly.

"Did you wish for rain?" She breathed in the scent of his fruity shampoo.

"No." He pulled back to look at her, eyes bright. "I wished that you would stay for Christmas."

She pulled him close and tears slipped down her cheeks.

CHAPTER TWELVE

*T*he Land cruiser sludged through the wet dirt, spraying up mud and skidding the tyres. Paige gritted her teeth and silently prayed that they wouldn't get bogged and have to walk home in the rain.

Logan needed to check on the stock, bores and fences. Jess and the children had insisted on coming along and, even though she would have preferred to stay in her room, Scotty had dragged Paige along with them. They sat together in the back seat, animatedly bouncing around, without a care in the world.

"You guys okay back there?" Jess turned in her seat. Her blond hair was done up in a tight pony tail which swayed with the rhythm of the car.

The children ignored her and Paige gave her a tight smile. "Just fine, thanks."

Logan mumbled something under his breath and shifted into a lower gear.

"What's wrong?" Jess asked him in her sweet voice.

"There's something wrong with that cow." He pointed out the front window and Paige saw a cream-coloured creature laying on its side in the mud.

Logan pulled up to a stop near it. "Stay here," he ordered his children before climbing out into the warm rain.

Scotty climbed over his sisters and opened the door, scrambling out.

"Scotty." Paige sighed and followed after him.

When she reached Logan and his son she stopped abruptly, her hand flying to her mouth. Blood oozed from the torn, infected flesh.

Nausea overwhelmed her and she turned away just in time to vomit up her breakfast.

"What's wrong with it, Daddy?" Scotty asked. Paige wiped her mouth and looked over to see the boy prod at the beast with a stick.

"Please don't do that." Logan's voice was calm and controlled, everything Paige couldn't be right now.

"What happened to it?" She asked.

"Looks like a feral dog attacked it." Logan crouched down and stroked the cow's head. It snorted sadly it reply.

"It's still alive?" Paige pulled Scotty to her.

"Not for long. I'll have to go back and get the gun. I can't leave her like this."

"Gun? No gun!" Scotty struggled free from Paige's grasp. "I need my ear muffs."

Brooke, Layla and Jess had ventured over now and Logan moved to hide their view of the mauled animal.

"Ugh. What happened?" Layla looked around her father to see the creature.

Paige picked Brooke up in her arms. "Back to the car kids."

As she walked past Jess, she saw the deathly pale expression on the woman's face. At least she wasn't the only one deeply affected by the situation.

Scotty was covering his ears with his hands, shouting incessantly that he needed his ear muffs. Once the girls were safely in the car Paige stooped to his eye level and touched him. "Sweetheart, we're going home to get your earmuffs."

He moved his hands and looked back at her. His eyes were filled with panic and confusion. "Home?"

"Yes, we're going home. Hop in the car now." Scotty did as he was told and Paige looked back at Logan. He was leading Jess back to the car an arm around her shoulder.

They were silent on the trip back.

Once safely home the girls ran off to tell their grandparents and Jess disappeared to the safety of the guest room.

Paige watched as Scotty approached his father. "Why do you need the gun?"

Logan looked pleadingly at Paige. She moved to stand beside him for support.

"That animal has been hurt." Logan explained. "It's in a lot of pain."

"What hurt it?"

"A dog tried to eat it."

Scotty's eyes widened. "Why? Was it hungry?"

"Maybe. But it didn't kill it and now I have to."

"Why? Can't you call the vet?"

"It's too late for a vet."

Paige opened her arms to her young charge as tears streamed down his cheeks. She made sure to hug him with just enough reassuring pressure. His body soon eased into hers and relaxed.

Paige looked at Logan's broken face. "Go, do it."

He nodded and left them alone together. She closed her eyes as she imagined him unlocking the gun cabinet and lifting out a rifle. The animal would be out of its pain soon.

CHAPTER THIRTEEN

*L*ogan really didn't want to go out. If the rain hadn't eased he would have declared it unsafe driving weather. But they had two good four-wheel drive vehicles so there was really no excuse not to drive the sixteen kilometres to their neighbour's house. Beside Hugh and Ruth were really looking forward to it. The kids were too. There would be other children there for them to play with and they didn't often get the chance to socialise with others.

"Zip me up?" Jess asked turning her naked back to him. He pulled up the zip of her black dress and she twirled around for him. It showed off her body, which, he knew was exactly why she wore it. She kept trying to tempt him with kisses and caresses but he kept turning her down. It just didn't feel right.

"So how much longer will Paige be with us? I mean,

the kids must be able to start boarding school soon?" she asked as she brushed her hair.

Logan buttoned up his shirt. "They can't board for a few more years yet and I haven't really thought about it."

"Surely boarding school would be easier than having a govie around?"

"Not really. Boarding school is expensive and we can't afford that sort of cost. The rain may have started but we've just had a long drought and there's debt to pay back."

Jess swung around to him. "But you own so much land."

"Just because we have land doesn't mean we're rich." Frustration rose in him and his voice it was short. "Why are you asking these questions?"

"I want to understand our situation, my love." She slipped her arms around his waist.

"Our situation? This doesn't really involve you." He stiffened at her touch.

"Come on. We're practically engaged, we've been going out for ages."

He stepped away from her, his temper heightened. "I don't remember proposing or giving you a ring."

"Now, now don't get angry. I was just raising the subject." She turned to study herself in the mirror.

Ruth called out that it was time to leave.

"We'll talk about this when we get back." He opened

the door for her. She sent him an innocently sweet smile as she walked past him.

Paige was trying to be positive. Helen, and a few other govies and mums she knew from the school of the air, would be at the party tonight and she would be happy to talk to them again.

She'd dressed in a long blue shirt and white floaty skirt. The rain although a welcome relief brought with it muggy humidity she wasn't used too.

She had been avoiding Logan and Jess but had glimpsed them getting into the Land cruiser behind them. Logan looked handsome in his jeans and plaid shirt. Jess was wearing a too-short tight dress. Not the best example for Layla and Brooke who were such impressionable young girls.

Once they arrived at the Henderson's place, Paige took the children off to find their friends.

It didn't take long to find Helen and they immediately sat down to catch up...

"How's this heat?" Helen wiped her forehead with her sleeve.

"I know. But the rain is great." They were sitting on the wide porch as the kids played on bikes and scooters on the concreted area.

"Are you going home when the roads clear?" Helen asked.

"I was supposed to be home for Christmas. What about you?"

"I'm staying. I've started dating Mick, one of the ringers here. Besides, I couldn't do an English winter after this."

Paige was pleased for her friend, but still heart-broken over Logan. "I don't think I will come back next year."

"What? Why not?"

"Logan's girlfriend Jess has come to stay. I heard they're getting married." Paige looked through the window beside them and could see Jess chatting flirta-tiously with another young man.

"Is that her? She's so young."

Paige described what had happened at the play-ground and how Jess had shown up at the house.

"You like him," Helen said softly.

Paige paused before nodding slightly.

A familiar country song started playing and people gathered on the makeshift dance floor inside.

"Come on. We may as well enjoy ourselves instead of moping around out here."

Paige let Helen lead her inside where immediately swept up in the dancing crowd.

She enjoyed the music, even if it was country and western, and danced with her friend until her feet were sore.

As a slow song started, someone tugged gently on her arm. In the low light Logan's face was mostly in shadow, but she knew it was him by his familiar, outback man smell.

"Dance with me?" he murmured into her ear. Her skin tingled as his warm breath brushed her skin.

Paige moved into the curve of his body as he placed her hands on his chest. She felt his heart pounding beneath her fingertips. His left hand curved around her back and held her in place as they swayed sideways. His right hand gently stroked her bare forearm.

Overwhelmed by the emotions rolling through her, Paige lay her head against his shoulder and closed her eyes. Everything else disappeared as she melted into the music and the rhythm of their slow dance.

All too quickly the music changed. Paige reluctantly lifted her head and their eyes met. His were a mixture of emotion and anguish. She opened her mouth to say something but he placed a finger to her lips then gently kissed her forehead.

Cool air rushed into the space he left as he walked away through the crowd and she watched Jess pounce on him, planting an exaggerated kiss on his lips.

Paige turned away from the crowd and slipped outside. It was time to leave the outback.

"We're taking the kids home." Ruth shouted over the thumping country music.

Logan nodded and looked around the room for

Paige. He hadn't seen her since their dance. Their emotion-charged, amazing dance.

"She's in the Land cruiser with Scotty." Ruth answered his unspoken question. "You finish up here and head home when you're ready." His mother winked at him and touched his cheek briefly before turning and leaving the party.

He heard Jess before he saw her. She was the life of the party. With a bourbon and coke in her hand, certainly not her first for the night, she was loudly singing along to the crooning, country song while moving her body in a sexy swagger. Men, young and old danced around her but he noticed young Brendon Macmillan paying her particular interest. Brendon was Jess's age and had the same outgoing nature as she did. They would make an ideal couple. Plus, Logan thought, Brendon came from money.

Taking a deep breath, Logan tapped Jess on the shoulder and motioned for her to come with him. She pouted but let him lead her away.

Outside the breeze was pleasantly cool on his skin.

"We should head home."

"You go. I'm having a good time." She gulped from her drink. "I don't think this is going to work out anyway."

Taken aback, Logan frowned. "What?"

"You and me. You just can't give me what I need." Her words were slurred but full of truth.

"You're right, Jess. I can't. I'm sorry." He feigned

remorse, but inside he was ecstatic. He hadn't wanted to hurt her by breaking up with her, but now she was breaking up with him.

"Brendon is a great guy. You should give him a go."

Jess looked inside. Brendon was watching them nervously.

"That govie of yours." She looked up at him, her eyes clear and sober. "I think she wants to be more than just your governess." Jess lifted her can at him. "Merry Christmas."

Logan watched her walk back inside and take Brendon's hand.

With new purpose, Logan said his goodbyes and headed home for Christmas.

CHAPTER FOURTEEN

*C*hristmas Day started the same as any other day. The sun rose behind the rain clouds and brought with it a searing summer heat.

Paige dressed, then Skyped her family in Melbourne. They were disappointed she wouldn't be there but she promised to fly home as soon as the rain stopped and the roads cleared.

With boots on, Paige waded through the puddles to the homestead. The rain had eased to a light drizzle. She would check on the road conditions, hopefully she would be able to leave soon.

The children were already inspecting the parcels under the tree as Ruth and Hugh worked in the kitchen making breakfast.

"Merry Christmas." She smiled as the kids ran to her with hugs and kisses.

"Santa came." Brooke pointed to the tree they had

decorated the week before. It was artificial, unlike the heavy scented trees you could get in cooler climates.

"Wow, what a lot of presents." Paige let the children lead her to the tree and watched as they sorted the wrapped gifts into piles.

She turned at Logan's heavy footsteps. His hair was messed and she wondered if he had slept any better. Their eyes met briefly before she turned away.

Ruth pushed a cup into his hand. "Good morning, dear. Did everything get sorted out last night?"

Ruth gave another cup to Paige and she sipped at the hot tea.

"It did." He nodded and turned to Paige. "Can I borrow you for a minute?"

"Who wants pancakes?" Hugh put a plate piled high with fluffy pancakes on the table and the kids rushed noisily to the table, presents forgotten.

"Later," Paige said as she past him on the way to the table.

As she helped cut up food and pour on syrup she wondered if he was going to apologise for the dance. Maybe he was going to fire her. Well, she was going to quit anyway so what did it matter?

After the pancakes were devoured they all sat around opening presents. Jess was mysteriously absent and Paige wondered if she was still sleeping. No one asked and she didn't want to be the one to bring it up. A spark of hope ignited inside her.

Brooke was thrilled with her boxes of Barbie dolls

and dress up clothes. Scotty got a pile of books and Layla got paints and brushes which she couldn't wait to start using.

The adults received presents too and, although she wasn't expecting anything, Paige was presented with a box. When she opened it, she found a hand painted mug with the words World's Best Govie on it.

Tears stung her eyes as she hugged each of the children.

Once the presents were over and the cleaning up finished, Paige put her boots back on and rushed through the rain to her donga. She hadn't been there more than a few minutes when there was a knock on the screen door.

"Paige."

She turned to see Logan dripping wet on her small porch.

Her breath caught. "What are you doing here? Get out of the rain." She opened the door for him and they stood together in the door way.

"I need to talk to you." His eyes were wide and vulnerable.

"You don't need to sack me," she said. "I've already decided not to come back."

"What? No, we need you." His voice trembled.

"But, Jess?"

"Jess and I are finished. I don't even know why we were ever together." He scratched his head. "I can't be with her when I'm in love with someone else."

She looked deeply into his eyes, hazy with desire and as he looked back at her she leaned against him slipping her arms around his neck, her heart thudding against his chest. Their kiss was full of all the love and desire they held for the other.

Whistles and laughter had them breaking away and turning to the house. The window was wide and they saw Ruth, Hugh and all the kids smiling widely at them, cheering them on.

"About bloody time.," Hugh called.

Paige looked back at Logan. "I love you too."

"Will you stay with us?" he asked, "As more than a govie?"

Paige wanted to pinch herself. Was this really happening? Was it possible to be this happy?

She kissed him again, and again, and again.

EPILOGUE

 year later

The homestead still smelled of fresh paint and was decorated with tinsel and lights. A green and red wreath that Layla had made hung on the front door, welcoming family and guests.

The wet season had come early this year but clear, warm weather was forecast for Christmas Day.

Paige looked out the bedroom window at the new buildings that had been erected next to her school house. Her family and close friends from Victoria were staying in there, having come up for the big day.

"You look amazing," her father said and she turned to see him dab at his eyes.

"Thank you." She hugged him, careful not to smudge her makeup. "It means so much to us that you're here.

"I wouldn't miss this for the world."

She looked around the bedroom she shared with Logan. She turned back to the mirror and smiled. The long white dress had been her mother's and had been altered only slightly to fit her. The delicate veil had been her Nona's brought with her from Italy. It was her something old and borrowed.

So much had changed this past year. Hugh's health had stabilised and he had semi-retired, allowing the new station manager and Logan to do all the heavy lifting and hard work these days.

Logan still worked at the mines on a week on, week off roster. He loved his job and wasn't ready to give up the money and job security for a life on the station. The wage he bought home still paid most of the bills and Paige knew he loved working on the big machinery. He had given up going to the pub. When he wasn't on Skype with his family, he spent his down time playing footy with his mates or working out in the gym.

As for herself she was still teaching the kids in the school room. Despite the change in situation their education was still a huge priority and she wouldn't allow anything to get in the way of that.

"It's time," her father said and offered his arm.

Layla and Brooke walked ahead, both stunning in

their cream-coloured dresses, each holding a bouquet of yellow daisies. Paige smiled at Scotty in his special suit holding the ring pillow carefully in his hands.

Walking through the house and out into the newly-planted garden, Paige smiled at her cousins, aunts and uncles.

As she passed Helen they shared a knowing look. Her friend was still at the Henderson's station and was in the process of applying for permanent residency. She had found her home here in the outback too.

Other families and friends they had met through distance education also sat in the guest's seats. Each term they had attended a mini-school camp in Longreach where they ran activities and classes. Paige had made more friends and met other resilient outback mums and governesses.

Her Nona, Mother and brother, Antonio stood in the front row watching the procession. Both women wore wide smiles and had tear-filled eyes. Antonio grinned and winked at her.

She breathed in the fresh country air before turning her gaze to her fiancé.

Logan stood waiting for her, freshly shaved and gazing adoringly at her. Her father handed her over with a kiss for her, and a handshake for Logan.

Logan took her hands in his and leaned in to whisper in her ear. "You'll always have a home here with us. You're not a govie anymore."

She smiled, blissfully in love. With him, with the children and the station. She may have come for a job, but here, with them, she had found her true home.

Thank you so much for reading The Outback Governess. I hope you enjoyed this sweet journey to love. For more information about me and my books, including the inspiration behind my stories, how I help other authors, and plenty of other fun stuff visit my website. If you'd like to know when my next release becomes available, plus gain access to exclusive content, news and giveaways, please sign up to my newsletter via my website and social media:

www.facebook.com/sarahwilliamswriter
www.twitter.com/SarahW_Writer
www.sarahwilliamsauthor.com

Help others find their next read by leaving a review of this novel on your favourite book website.

Keep an eye out for my future story where we will catch up with Paige's brother Antonio...

Read on for a sneak peak of *The Brothers of Brigadier Station*

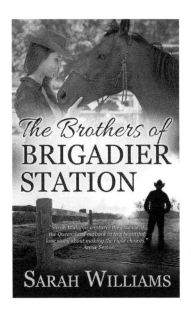

She came to the outback to marry the love of her life. She just didn't expect him to be her fiancé's younger brother.

When Meghan Flanagan, a vet-nurse from Townsville, moves to Brigadier Station in outback Queensland to marry the man of her dreams, she is shocked to discover that perhaps her fiancé isn't the man she wants waiting for her at the altar. The man she's destined to marry, just might be his younger brother.

Cautious of women after a disastrous past relationship, Darcy is happy living on his beloved cattle station, spending his spare time riding horses, going to rodeos and campdrafting. He didn't expect the perfect woman show up on his doorstep. Engaged to his brother.

With the wedding only hours away, Meghan must make the decision of a lifetime. But, her betrayal could tear the family apart. She knows all too well the pain of losing loved ones and being alone.

Now that she has the family she so desperately wants; will she risk losing it all?

CHAPTER ONE

*S*ettle down, boy." Meghan coaxed the huge German Shepherd, using all of her strength to keep the great beast on the cold, metal table.

"Almost done, just a little longer." Jennifer, the veterinarian, called from the end where the dog's great head lay as his owner watched.

Having your teeth checked at the dentist was never a pleasant experience, so Meghan couldn't blame the old dog for being agitated. She held chunks of its sweaty fur in her fists. It stank of dirt and urine. It had probably gotten anxious in the car ride and wet himself. Owners never told them that. It was common to find wet patches on the animals that visited Spotty Dogz Vet Surgery.

Still, in all her years working as a vet nurse, being wet on wasn't her worst experience. She was often a scratching post for vicious cats and had lost count of the numerous bites from a variety of rodents and birds. Her pain threshold had increased dramatically since she had finished her training. There were other parts of the job that were far worse. Like caring for a cat who was in constant, agonizing pain or having an innocent young puppy die in her arms. Those experiences left a mark that couldn't be seen.

While healthy, domestic animals were cute and adorable, but it was the larger animals, especially horses, that Meghan wanted to work with.

"All done." Jennifer stepped back. The dog hurled itself out of Meghan's grasp and off the table. Claws scrapping on the metal surface.

Jennifer and the owner tackled the creature out of the room, leaving Meghan alone to clean the instruments and sterilize the table. After washing her hands, she visited her patients. A new litter of short haired, tabby kittens had been brought in after being found abandoned. Meghan had already checked the kittens for fleas and ticks when they had first arrived yesterday, now they were just waiting for microchipping and vaccinations. A brown and grey boy cried mournfully and Meghan couldn't help wishing she could adopt them all. She scooped up the tiny kitten and snuggled it against her chin. Its soft fur tickled her skin and its small heart thumped against her fingertips.

After a few minutes of loving, she placed the kitten back with his siblings, stroking all six in turn, saying a quiet goodbye and hoping they all found good homes before her next shift.

She sighed as she glanced at her watch, it was almost the end of her shift. It had been a long day and she was looking forward to spending the night on the couch with her fiancé, Lachie. He had only arrived yesterday from his home in the outback and she had barely seen him yet.

Her phone buzzed in her back pocket. She pulled it out and answered when her best friend's name appeared.

"Hey, Jodie," a smile tugged at the corners of her mouth. Jodie could always make her feel better.

"Are you still at work?"

"Yeah. Almost over."

"I just wanted to wish you luck for tomorrow. What time are you leaving?"

"First thing. Lachie said it takes about seven hours plus breaks."

"Geez, what a long drive. Did you really have to fall for a guy who lives on a farm in the outback?"

Meghan laughed. "It's a cattle station, not a farm. It's been in the family for generations so he didn't get much of a choice where it was."

Jodie was quiet, but Meghan knew her friend well enough to know when she was rolling her eyes.

"Well, good luck meeting his family. Use these two weeks to make sure moving out there is what you really want."

"I will." Meghan's eyes prickled with threatening tears. "I'm going to miss you. We've been friends for what… twenty years? We've never been apart this long."

"It's going to be harder if you move out there permanently."

After the wedding, Meghan would call the station home. Leaving her best friend wouldn't be the only thing she would miss about Townsville. The beach, the food, the music. But the country promised excitement; a new start, a new identity, the family she longed for. She would become Mrs. Lachlan McGuire of Brigadier Station. She bit her lip, containing a grin. His country upbringing had been appealing right from the start. He was outgoing and confident. The fact that he was gorgeous helped too.

"Call me. I want updates. And photos. Find out about the other brothers. If either are single and hot, I want to know." Jodie was always keeping an eye out for her next boyfriend.

"I will. Love you."

"Love you too. Safe trip."

Meghan slipped her phone back in her trousers and glanced at her watch again. After her rounds, it would be time to say goodbye and her two-week holiday would start. She would finally meet Lachie's Mum and brother and see where he lived and had grown up. They would also be announcing their engagement.

At twenty-nine, Meghan Flanagan was about to have everything she had ever wanted. She was in love and moving to the country to start a new life. A better life. She had never been happier.

The television was blaring when Meghan got home. The air smelled musty when she stepped into the kitchen. She placed the bags on the kitchen counter and opened a window, allowing a cool breeze to waft in. She peeked into her small living room. Lachlan McGuire was sprawled on the couch, beer in hand, watching the North Queensland Cowboys defend their title. He was relaxed and happy. She knew he liked spending time in her modest little house. Away from the station, he could ignore the paperwork and bills that were no doubt overloading his email account; he worked hard, so Meghan couldn't blame him wanting to take a break.

"What's the score?"

He looked up and grinned the grin that made her insides quiver. "Cowboys are up by twelve."

Cowboys games always reminded her of when she had met Lachie eight months earlier. Jodie had dragged her to a home game. By sheer good fortune, they had been seated next to each other. Lachie had quickly won her over with his good looks and charm. She had been surprised by the attention. Gorgeous guys didn't waste their time on plain girls like her. She wondered if he was being nice to her to get to Jodie. The tall, blonde beauty was often the centre of attention. But when the game was over, he asked for Meghan's number and within a week they were an item. Whenever she asked him why he had chosen her, he always replied: 'You're a girl I can take home to Mum.'

"Is that Thai food I smell?" He climbed off the couch and followed his nose to the kitchen.

"I got that Pad Thai you like." She watched as he opened containers appreciatively and started serving it up onto two plates.

Meghan moved into the sitting room, kicked off her shoes and curled up on the couch before turning the TV volume down with the remote.

"Did you do anything exciting today?" She called out as she waited for Lachie.

"Nah, just hung out here. Watched some TV." He carried the plates back to the living room to join her on the couch, balancing his plate on his knees.

"How was work?"

She shrugged. "I always liked my job, but now it's gotten so repetitive. I'm ready for a change."

"I reckon you'll love the country. Lots of wide open spaces and you're a country girl at heart." He winked at her before scooping a generous forkful of food into his mouth.

She had heard so much about their sprawling cattle property in the outback and his beloved mother.

"I'm nervous, I've never met a guy's Mum before."

"Mum's a treat. Don't be scared of her. Did you talk to Jodie today?"

"She called me at work and assured me it'll be okay."

"It will and this visit is only for a couple of weeks. After the wedding, we can still come visit once a year or so."

She looked into his blue eyes and smiled. Her future was so full of hope and possibilities, it was exciting and a little frightening.

"I love you, Lachie. I can't wait to start our life together."

His lips brushed gently over hers causing warmth to pool in her belly.

She would meet his mother and brother tomorrow and she would finally see the property. Her future home.

Brigadier Station.

CHAPTER TWO

*C*racked brown dirt stretched flat in every direction. The occasional ironbark tree provided the only shelter from the harsh elements of the North Queensland outback.

Although Meghan had never been this far from the coast before, she knew in her heart she would love the country and quickly adjust to living on the land. It had been a long drive from Townsville, passing through the small township of Charters Towers then the smaller, communities of Hughenden and Richmond. In these places, she had learnt of the abundant dinosaur fossils which were often found in the hard earth.

Now on the final stretch of dusty road between Julia Creek and Brigadier Station, she decided the stark, austere scenery was, surprisingly, quite beautiful.

"Don't worry," Lachie glanced at her as his ute rattled over a cattle-grid. "Brigadier isn't as bare as these stations. We've got plenty of shade and good bores.

"So, you're doing okay despite the drought?" Meghan had heard plenty of stories about how hard the outback graziers were doing it in this drought. Cattle were starving to death and many owners were killing their own stock rather than see their beasts suffer.

Lachie had grown up on the cattle station and had inherited it when his father died a few years ago. He had told her what to expect and she was more than up for the challenge.

"Well, we manage. It's not easy, though. Lots of hard work."

Meghan admired his profile. His trim and toned body were the result of that hard, physical work. The sleeves of his grey work shirt rolled up above his long, suntanned forearms. Meghan was shorter by a foot, but he towered over most people at his lofty six-foot-four height.

"What?" He caught her watching him. "You checking me out?"

She giggled flirtatiously. "So, what if I am?"

He wiggled his eyebrows at her. "I can always pull the ute over."

She crinkled her nose and gestured to the tools and machinery parts at her feet and between them.

"There's not enough room in here to move. Remember the last time we did it in here?"

His deep chuckle sent a shiver down her spine as it always did.

"Good point. But I do have my swag in the back." He gestured behind him to the tray, where her suitcase was tied down.

"That stinky old thing? I love you, but no thanks."

Winding the window down she let the warm air blow on her face, whipping her long hair about as they sped down the road. She gazed over the land, barren and deserted.

She hoped Lachie's family liked her. Especially his mum—a woman he admired and loved. Would she be hard and stern, like this land? Disappointed that her oldest son was with a city girl? Or would she be accepting and kind? Weren't country people supposed to be friendly?

"Don't be nervous."

She looked over and realised she had been gnawing on her bottom lip.

"That obvious?"

"There's no need. Mum will love you." He reached over and patted her knee briefly. "I'll tell her about the engagement at dinner. After she gets to know you a bit."

"I hope she approves." She rubbed her sweaty hands over her jeans. Lachie had proposed over pizza last weekend. It hadn't been a passionate gesture. He didn't even have a ring. But she had been delighted, throwing herself into his arms. That she might not be cut out for remote country life hadn't occurred to her. She loved the idea of wide-open space, animals, country quiet, and of course she loved Lachie.

They soon pulled into a gravelled driveway, marked only by a worn wooden sign attached to the fence that read Brigadier Station. Meghan straightened in her seat as the homestead appeared. Excitement curled in her stomach; it was just as she had imagined it would be. Set on higher ground with sloping views across the brown paddocks, the modest, cream coloured building had a veranda that wrapped around the front of the house, creating lots of comfortable nooks to take in the view.

Lachie parked the ute in a vacant spot in an old shed, next to a four-wheel drive and a tractor. As she climbed out of her seat, she wrinkled her nose as the aroma of hay and molasses wafted by. Familiar farm smells that brought back her earliest childhood memories. Meghan whirled around. Carefully pruned rose bushes stood proudly in the front garden beds. Strolling over to a bush burdened with white rose buds she touched the soft petals with her fingertips and inhaled their sweet fragrance.

"It's nice to see another woman appreciating my roses."

Startled, she looked over at the tall, older woman who had appeared by her side.

"I'm not much of a gardener, but I love flowers, roses in particular. I didn't think they grew out here."

"These are a hardy variety. My mother-in-law planted them before my time and showed me how to keep them going before she died. She was a cranky old lady, but she knew her stuff. She taught me a lot."

"Mum." Lachie bent down and hugged his mother with his free arm.

"Already giving Meghan gardening advice, I see."

Meghan offered her hand. "It's lovely to meet you, Mrs. McGuire."

Harriet's accepting hand was warm and soft. "Call me Harriet, honey. We're not formal out here."

Harriet McGuire had a face that looked like she laughed easily and often. Her shoulder-length hair was streaked with grey and had been cut by someone with a good eye for style. Behind her glasses were eyes just as blue as her son's. Harriet placed an arm around Meghan's back and led her inside.

"It'll be fun to have another woman in the house for a while. Gets a bit rowdy with two boys here."

"That wouldn't surprise me." Meghan grinned, touched by such a warm welcome.

Lachie dropped their bags haphazardly in the hallway before giving her a quick kiss.

"Just going to check the emails. Mum will help you settle in." Before either woman could object, he was disappearing down the hallway.

"He'll be busy for a while, I'm afraid." Harriet directed Meghan through the small but practical kitchen and into the larger living room.

"That's what happens when he takes time off. But I'm glad you could come back with him this time."

"I'm glad I could finally join him. Work has been so busy."

"Make yourself comfortable. I'll put the kettle on, then you can tell me all about yourself."

She slipped out of the room leaving Meghan to wander around the living room.

The inside of the house was every bit as welcoming as the outside. The walls were filled with photographs, and she took them all in, absorbing the family history. There were several black-and-white wedding photos and portraits of elegant men and women. She recognized Harriet in her wedding photo with her late husband. What had Lachie said his name was? David? No, Daniel. They were both attractive and looked good together.

The modern photos were all of the same three boys. A picture of them together caught her eye, and she studied it. The boys wore swimming shorts, and were sitting on a rock in a river, their hair wet. They looked similar with light brown hair and bright blue eyes. Meghan recognized Lachie and guessed him to be about ten in the photo.

Harriet reappeared and came to stand next to her.

"Those are the Brothers of Brigadier Station. They've been getting called that since they were little," she explained. "Did you recognize Lachie?"

Meghan nodded. "He's the oldest one."

"That's right. The one next to him is my youngest, Noah, he lives in New Zealand now. And that's Darcy." She pointed to the slim little boy in the picture, her voice softening. "He's still here. He's saving money to buy his own property one day."

"They all have your beautiful blue eyes."

"Yes, they are a good-looking bunch. Temperamental at times, but I'm proud of them. Lachie's had lots of responsibility put on him since Daniel died. He wasn't expecting to inherit Brigadier's until he was much older. Darcy has helped a lot with the workload which lets Lachie visit you in Townsville." Harriet smiled widely at her visitor. "Come, the jug's boiled."

Meghan followed her to the kitchen where she made cups of tea and set the table with freshly baked scones, strawberry jam, and cream.

"I hope you like it here."

"I love it so far. I can't wait to see more of the station."

Meghan topped her scone with jam and took a bite. It was still warm and melted in her mouth. "It's been a long time since I've had homemade scones and these are delicious."

"Thank you. I'm glad you like them."

Meghan was surprised to find out they had much in common despite the generational gap as they continued chatting. Harriet admitted to reading voraciously. "I like to support Australian writers in particular."

"Me too." Meghan sipped her tea. She found it comforting that Harriet, a woman born and raised in the country, would be an avid reader.

"Do your parents live in Townsville too?"

Meghan's shoulders slumped slightly. "My Dad died before I started school and Mum passed away in a car accident two years ago."

Harriet's voice softened. "I'm so sorry for your loss."

"Thank you. They were great people, and I miss them so much. Especially Mum, we were very close."

Tears threatened as they always did when talking about her family, but she pushed them back.

"Mum would have liked you."

"I'm sure I would have liked her too." Harriet sipped her tea. "Do have any other family? Brothers or sisters?"

"No, Mum never remarried. She was happy with her teaching career. She taught at one of the Catholic schools in Townsville. I have a best friend, Jodie, she's like family."

As they finished off their tea, the phone rang, and Harriet glanced at it. "I'll get the phone. When you're ready, you can go and unpack."

Downing the last of her black tea, a drink she would have to get used to as no one else drank coffee, Meghan collected her bags and went in search of Lachie's bedroom. All the bedrooms came off the same long hallway, and Lachie's appeared the first on her right. She knew it was his by the familiar, dirty clothes scattered on the floor. Obviously, Harriet didn't pick up after him. Meghan smiled; she'd given up the hope he would start being tidier.

His room was large, taken up by a king-size bed and matching dresser. Meghan put her bag on the bed and considered changing out of her jeans and T-shirt.

But, curiosity got the better of her, and she left the room and wandered further down the hall. She found two more bedrooms similar to Lachie's but without the mess; the bathroom, and a separate toilet. The large room at the end she presumed was Harriet's. A glance in told her she was right and, to her relief, she noticed an en-suite. At least she would only have to share a bathroom with Lachie and his brother.

After finding cupboards and the laundry, Meghan came to the office where Lachie sat, his chin resting in his palm as he scrutinized something on the computer screen.

"Hey, sexy," she purred as she came around to stand behind him and snuggled her head against his shoulder.

"Having fun?" He turned his head and kissed her cheek.

"Your Mum is on the phone. I found your room and put my bag in there. I presume we're sleeping together?"

"Yeah, Mum's cool with that. Do you want to see the horses?"

"Absolutely I do. You know I love horses."

"There's a path from the kitchen. Easy to find, past the chickens."

"You don't want to show me?"

He barely raised his eyes from the screen. "I'm sorry. I've got so much work to do."

Disappointed, but excited to explore, she took off in the direction he had said.

≈

The dirt path stretched beside a row of young coolabah trees, past the chicken coop and down to a wooden stable. Meghan spotted a chestnut horse's head peeking out over a metal railing. Cautiously, she stretched out her hand so it could sniff her, then stroked its head gently when it appeared friendly. The long-forgotten smell of horse assailed her nostrils.

"Oh, aren't you a handsome boy! What's your name?" she cooed.

"Thank you for the compliment, but if you're talking to the horse, I don't know if she would appreciate being called handsome." The warm, masculine voice coming from behind the horse surprised her. She jumped back, lost her footing and landed butt first on the dirt floor. The stranger walked around and stopped abruptly when he saw her.

He must be the brother.

Heat filled her cheeks as she pushed herself back to standing and wiped at the back of her pants. She focused her gaze on his dirty jeans and the dark brown of his work boots. "I'm sorry, I didn't know you were in here."

"It's okay, I don't get to hear compliments that often." He sounded amused.

"I meant the horse," she stuttered. "S-she's beautiful."

"Yes, she is." His voice was soft.

Meghan tucked her hair behind her ear nervously, then looked up into his deep blue eyes. "Darcy, right?"

"And you must be Lachie's girlfriend." His easy smile produced a dimple on his unshaven cheek.

"Meghan." She tried to calm her pounding heart. What was wrong with her? Yes, he was ruggedly good looking, similar to Lachie but rougher and with a squarer jawline. Something about Darcy captured her gaze and refused to release it.

A small black and white dog appeared beside him and yelped for attention, breaking the moment.

"And who are you?" She smiled at the fox terrier.

"This is my dog, Joey. Go ahead he won't bite."

Bending down, she extended her hand for the dog to sniff. After a brief glance at his owner, the canine trotted over for a scratch.

She could feel Darcy watching her. She stood up and looked about the barn, but her eyes soon came back to rest on him.

Darcy shook his head, breaking the contact and pointed to a shelf behind her. "Can you hand me a brush, please?"

Meghan turned and surveyed an array of brushes, combs, and hoof picks before choosing one and handing it over, careful not to touch him. He nodded in thanks.

She turned her attention back to the mare. "She's a lovely horse."

He brushed the horse with long strokes. "This is Shadow. She's pregnant. Due in a week or so. That's why she's not in the paddock with the others."

Meghan stepped back. The mare's belly was protruding, full with foal. She stroked it, and the baby inside rewarded her with a gentle kick against her hand.

"Do you ride?" He bent to brush the mare's legs, his denim clad buttocks caught her gaze.

She averted her eyes to a comb, grabbing it she began working on the horse's mane.

"I was born on a station near Charters Towers. My dad bred horses.

Mum used to say I was riding before I learnt how to walk." She smiled at the memory. "I remember sitting in front of my dad. He used to let me hold the reins."

"And you live in Townsville now?"

"Yep. Dad died when I was little, and we had to sell up and move."

Meghan remembered her early years on the station. Her mother and father still young and deeply in love, working side by side with the horses while she watched from a safe distance. A feeling of complete happiness and serenity enveloping her. Those years remained the happiest time of her life.

"I'm sorry to hear that. I know what it's like to lose a father," Darcy sympathized.

"It was a long time ago." After her father had died, her mother had mourned him for years. Meghan had struggled at school both academically and socially. The small unit they had moved to was claustrophobic, and the moist heat of summer was suffocating. Eventually, she had grown used to it, but the yearning for the country life had remained. Now, finally back on the land, she could almost feel the dust settling back into her veins.

Darcy's gravelly voice pulled her back to the present. "So, what do you think of Brigadier Station?"

"I haven't seen much of it yet. It's very dry and dusty."

"Yep. Queensland's dust bowl. We need a good wet season."

"I can imagine it's even more beautiful when it's green," she smiled, envisioning long green grass where cracked brown dirt lay shrivelling more every day.

"The drought will break someday," Darcy said surely. "Nothing lasts forever."

CHAPTER THREE

*D*arcy watched Meghan with interest. She had a natural tenderness towards the mare. Her country upbringing was apparent in her confidence and ability as she expertly combed the horse's mane.

She was undoubtedly attractive, but instead of the blonde, high maintenance city girl with big boobs and little brains that were Lachie's usual choice, she was shorter and dark-haired. Tight blue jeans accentuated curvy hips. Memories of his ex-girlfriend briefly invaded his thoughts. He shook his head, ridding himself of unpleasant memories.

Darcy continued brushing his horse. His gaze frequently coming back to the woman beside him. Occasionally she would ask a question which he would answer with his usual honesty, but even when neither of them spoke there was a strange easiness between them.

"We should head back. Dinner's probably ready by now." He placed the tack back on the shelf and gestured for her to lead the way. She waited as he bolted the stable door in place behind them, keeping the mare safe inside.

"Thanks for letting me help. Please tell me if I get in your way," Meghan said as they walked side by side back to the house.

He turned to her, his mouth set in a straight line, his gaze steady on her. "I will. And just so you know, I never lie. Not to anyone." If there was one thing he hated, it was secrets and lies. He'd seen what damage they could cause, and was not about to repeat the sins of his father.

Meghan bit her bottom lip. As he studied the lines in her lips, he wondered about their softness.

Joey barked and ran up to the house. Darcy watched as his mother greeted the dog at the door.

"Come on. I smell dinner." They started walking back up the path.

Darcy couldn't imagine Meghan getting in his way. In fact, it might be nice to have a young woman around the place for a few days, especially if she could keep Lachie in line. God knows he needed it.

~

Meghan breathed in the cooler evening air and gazed across the brown plains. Lachie and Darcy were relaxing next to her in wicker chairs spaced out on the veranda specially to enjoy the evening sunsets. Both men had their long, denim-clad legs stretched out in front, a cold beer in hand.

Harriet came out and took the vacant seat closest to Meghan. A ready smile on her face.

"What work do you do in Townsville?"

"I'm a vet nurse at a surgery. We mainly see cats and dogs." Meghan sipped her beer, the crisp ale washing away her nerves.

"You must really love animals then." Harriet leaned towards her. The faint smell of perfume lingered, reminding Meghan of the similar scent her mother had worn.

"I've always loved animals. But it's hard work. I really only see sick or abandoned pets, which is hard." Even talking about it choked her up and she swallowed back the emotions. "I'd like to learn more about cattle and horses."

"You'll certainly get a chance to do that here."

Lachie leant forward to join the conversation. "She's also a great photographer, Mum. You should see her work."

Meghan felt her cheeks warm. "I love photography. Painting too, but only as a hobby."

"I'd love to see some of your work. I'm sure you're very talented." Harriet patted her hand lightly. The familiar action surprised Meghan. She had forgotten what it was like to be part of a family.

"I see you brought your camera with you," Harriet nodded at the SLR on the coffee table. "Our sunsets are pretty spectacular."

"I'm always prepared."

"Speaking of." Darcy pointed to the huge orange disc hanging low in the Western sky. She snapped a continual stream of photos as the sun made its graceful descent below the horizon, streaking the sky red and orange for a few moments before darkness suddenly surrounded them.

"You don't see sunsets like that at home," Meghan breathed in awe as a cool breeze brushed her cheek.

"They are pretty spectacular," Darcy murmured.

"Come on then. I'm starving." Lachie's stomach growled in agreement.

Meghan collected her camera and followed the family inside to the dining room. She took the space next to Lachie while Darcy sat down opposite her.

Harriet's tender beef roast didn't disappoint. Meghan enjoyed every moist mouthful, unlike both the men who scoffed the meat and potatoes and picked at their greens.

"Seconds, Mum?" Lachie smiled sweetly.

Harriet nodded toward the bench. "There's plenty there. I cooked enough for sandwiches for the next few days too."

He stood and went to retrieve more.

"Do you ride any of the horses, Harriet?" Meghan asked, curious to see who Darcy had inherited his love of horses from.

"Not anymore. The horses are Darcy's. Lachie doesn't like horses. He prefers his motorbike." Harriet turned her attention to Darcy. "You should take Meghan. Molly's a sweet, gentle horse for a beginner."

Darcy glanced at Harriet. "Her dad used to breed horses."

"Really?" Lachie returned to his seat with his plate loaded up. "I didn't know that."

Meghan brushed the comment off. "Yes, we had a small property near Charters Towers, but we sold it when Dad got sick. I haven't ridden much since."

Darcy shifted slightly in his seat. "I need to do a bore run tomorrow if you want to come."

"That would be great. Thanks." Meghan smiled, eager for the chance to ride and explore the vast station. "You don't mind, do you, Lachie?"

He shook his head in reply.

"Now, Meghan," Harriet patted her hand gently, "Lachie has brought a couple of girls' home in the past, I won't lie."

"More than the couple you know about," Darcy teased quietly. His mother shushed him and continued. "He usually likes blondes."

"Mum!" Lachie protested.

"It's true. Darcy's the one who likes brunettes."

Meghan glanced across the table at Darcy. His sun-kissed skin had a touch of pink on it, but he avoided her gaze.

"Anyway, it's lovely to have you here, for the next couple of weeks." Harriet raised her wine glass in a toast.

"While we're toasting then, I should tell you that Meghan and I are engaged," Lachie announced.

Meghan's eyes widened. She had almost forgotten the reason for their trip. Her pulse raced as she took in the reactions. Darcy's eyebrows were raised in disbelief.

"Congratulations!" Harriet cried out, clapping her hands together.

Meghan stood to accept a warm hug, relief sweeping through her.

"I never thought this day would come!"

Darcy shook his brother's hand with a forced smile plastered on his face.

Lachie didn't seem to notice. He had a smug smile and a cheeky twinkle in his eye.

Darcy turned to her, his voice light with humour. "Sure you want to join this family? He's a handful." Darcy nodded at Lachie.

Meghan grinned. "I think I can handle it."

Harriet clapped her hands together. "We should be celebrating with champagne or something bubbly. I don't have anything, though."

"Beer will do." Darcy raised his bottle. "To the happy couple."

"To the happy couple." Harriet cheered as they all clinked their drinks together.

As the others sat down, Darcy pushed his chair in and gathered his plate.

"Where are you going?" Harriet asked.

"Gotta check on the horses." Meghan found Darcy's attention focused on the plates in his hands. "I'll be back late, so I'll say goodnight."

"Okay then. Good night." Harriet waved him off.

Harriet and Lachie dismissed him as if this behaviour were normal for Darcy. Meghan frowned at his excuse. They had already closed the stable for the evening. Why did he need to check on the horses again? She watched as he put his dishes in the sink and slipped quietly out of the house and into the chilly night.

"What's the deal with Darcy?" Meghan asked Lachie later as they were getting ready for bed. "Does he have a girlfriend?"

"Nah. He did in high school, but she did a number on him, and he hasn't dated much since."

"What did she do?"

"Who knows?" Lachie shrugged. "Darcy doesn't tell people much; he keeps to himself."

Meghan frowned and wondered what had happened. Darcy was good looking and would surely have women fighting over him if he lived in town. Perhaps he hadn't found one willing to live so remotely yet. Or perhaps he was a romantic and was holding out for true love. She liked the idea of that.

He must get lonely, though. She knew loneliness well enough.

She looked back at her fiancé. Lachie, Harriet, and Darcy were her family now. She couldn't have hoped for a better welcome or a better family to marry into.

Meghan woke to find the bed empty and sunshine streaming through the curtains. She had hoped that Lachie would wake her so they could have breakfast together. After quickly dressing in a pair of jeans and a T-shirt she headed to the kitchen.

"Good morning. How did you sleep?" Harriet stood at the kitchen counter kneading dough; the smell of baking filled the room.

"Amazingly well, thanks. Must be the fresh air."

"Good. The boys have left already and don't know when they'll be back. Help yourself to cereal and toast, or I can cook bacon and eggs for you."

"No, you're busy, and cereal sounds great." Meghan fixed her breakfast and chatted to Harriet while she ate. It had been a long time since she had enjoyed the company of an older woman and she was surprised how comfortable it was.

"I try to do a bunch of baking once a week. Bread, biscuits, and cakes. The boys like sweets for smoko."

"How far away is the supermarket?" Meghan polished off her Weetbix.

"There are two in Julia Creek, which is forty minutes away. But I only buy essentials from them or have them brought out on the mail run." Harriet adjusted the temperature on the oven in preparation for the next tray of Anzac biscuits. "I go west to Cloncurry once a month and do a big shop there."

"Cloncurry? Isn't that another couple of hours' drive?"

Harriet nodded. "That's why it's only once a month."

Meghan thought of Jodie. This was why she had insisted on her friend trying out country living before making such a huge move. They took things for granted in the city. Want a coffee? Go to a café. Want food delivered? No problem. Not out here. If you didn't have something in the fridge you couldn't just run down to the corner shop. Living out here was a whole different lifestyle.

"Don't you get lonely?"

Harriet gave her a knowing smile. "No, I'm in the Queensland Country Women's Association, and we meet regularly and fundraise, do art and craft, that sort of thing. Darcy has his camp-drafting. Lachie has his friends at the pub. Or he did before meeting you." Harriet wiped her hands on her apron and surveyed the counter. "We all support and help each other here. It's one of the best things about living in the country.

You have friends everywhere. Anyone can fit in as long as they want too."

Meghan washed up her bowl and put it away. Turning to Harriet her voice was hoarse with emotion. "Thank you. For such a warm welcome."

The strong, sugary smell of golden syrup enveloped her as Harriet put her arms around her. It held all the comfort of a mother's tender embrace. Meghan's eyes welled with unshed tears.

"This is your home now. Your family." The sincerity on Harriet's face was almost Meghan's undoing. She swiped at her eyes as she was released.

After a deep breath, she turned back to her new friend. "What can I do to help?"

"Would you mind getting the eggs for me from the chicken coop?"

"Sure." Meghan was happy to be useful, despite having never retrieved eggs from a coop before. Harriet pointed out the scrap bucket near the sink. "Feed them that too, please. The path is behind the rainwater tank."

Meghan followed the dirt path toward the large green tank. Last night she had learnt the family stored rainwater for bathing and cleaning.

Beside it was a pen with two large grunting pigs inside. They didn't look particularly friendly rooting around in the ground, so Meghan kept walking, spotting the henhouse a few feet further ahead.

The multi-coloured fowl were pecking at the grass

inside their large wire enclosure but looked up when they saw her approach. Meghan could feel their beady eyes fixed on her as she unlatched the door and entered, closing it behind her. She emptied the bucket of scraps on the ground, and the chickens flocked to the food clearing a path for her to move through. In the sheltered area, covered with slats of wood, she found individual boxes filled with straw. She collected each warm egg until she came upon a box that was still occupied by a ginger chook. Her feathers fluffed up, sharp curved beak ready to strike as its head twitched. Meghan chewed on her lip wondering if she should try to remove it.

After a failed attempt at trying to scare the hen, it shrilled angrily back at her in irritation.

It was just a chicken, after all. Nothing she couldn't handle.

Slowly she reached out her hand to get under the hen, when, suddenly it flew at her. Distracted by the whirlwind of feathers, Meghan felt a sudden pain in her hand.

"Ouch!" Meghan jumped back against the wall. The offending chicken looked at her, its head twitching from side to side, daring her to try that again.

"Okay, you win this round," she conceded. "But I'll win the war. Just wait and see."

To her surprise, the chicken casually jumped down from her nest and strutted out to join her friends.

Meghan exhaled in relief and collected the warm eggs before the hen changed her mind.

She fought the impulse to run back to the house after she locked the coop behind her. Looking around she was glad no one had witnessed the event.

"Well done," Harriet exclaimed when she saw the success. "Did any of them peck you?"

"Just the one." Meghan absentmindedly rubbed her hand.

"You've gotta show her who's boss." Harriet squeezed her arm reassuringly.

Darcy and Lachie arrived home just after one o'clock. Meghan's breath caught as she saw the pair for the first time that day. She couldn't help noticing how good they looked in their faded blue work shirts and worn jeans. It was the first time she had seen Lachie wearing a battered cowboy hat. It was pulled low on his head to protect him from the harsh burning sun. The whole effect of his appearance left her warm and tingling.

Lachie stopped long enough to kiss her cheek and whisper a good morning in her ear. His attention then focused on food. He was always hungry. She envied his metabolism.

The conversation over sandwiches was work focused and impersonal. Meghan tried to keep up but quickly lost interest in talk of machinery and fire breaks.

Lachie's phone rang and, throwing an apologetic smile her way, he answered it and walked off to his office. Harriet cleared up the dishes and disappeared back into the kitchen.

Meghan found herself alone with Darcy as they finished off their cups of tea. "Did you do anything exciting this morning?"

Darcy scratched his nose. "We repaired a fence. Thrilling stuff."

"Well, I collected eggs." She smiled proudly.

"Impressive. Did you get pecked?"

"Yes. Only by one."

"Congratulations. You've earned that ride." He finished off his tea, put his hat back on and headed for the door. "Come on."

She scrambled out of her chair and followed him outside. Hastily pulling her boots on at the door as Joey watched her, his tail wagging excitedly.

Shadow, the pregnant mare greeted her with a snort and Meghan quickly patted her as she followed Darcy, jogging to keep up with his long-legged stride. Through the stables there was a paddock where two horses roamed contentedly, their tails swishing at flies. A stocky brown pony trotted over and nudged Darcy's hand searching for treats.

"This is Molly." Darcy rubbed the pony's nose. Her age was evident from the greying hairs around her nostrils. "She's a softie. Mum brings her apples and spoils her."

Meghan patted her lovingly and tickled her chin. Molly closed her eyes enjoying the attention.

"Come on, girls," Darcy said as he led the way to the tack room. Swiftly with dexterous fingers, he saddled and bridled the mare while Meghan watched and befriended the horse. "She's an old girl, but she still loves a gallop. Just hold on if you lose control and I'll help you," he reassured her.

Meghan placed her foot in the stirrup, grabbed the saddle and hoisted herself up. He watched but refrained from helping. Once settled in her seat he adjusted the straps, his arm brushing her denim-clad calf.

Darcy handed her the reins and led her back out to the paddock. "Stay here. I'll be back in a minute."

Alone with the horse, she shuffled in her seat and got used to the feel of the hard saddle beneath her. It smelled freshly oiled. She held the reins. Molly's ears twitched but she stood silently, waiting for her commands. When she felt more confident, Meghan gave Molly a gentle kick and encouraged her to walk forward. The horse readily agreed, her gait smooth and fluid.

Instinct took over as together they walked around in circles, gradually increasing speed to a trot. Meghan matched the gentle rhythm, rising and fallen in time to the horse's gait.

"You're a natural." Darcy trotted over on a shiny black horse.

"It feels good to be back in the saddle."

"This is for you," he handed her an Akubra.

"Thanks." The fawn felt was smooth and new under her fingers. She put the hat on and pulled it low. It was a perfect fit. "What do you think?"

"You look like a cowgirl." His eyes trailed over her jeans, close fitting t-shirt, and brown boots. "Not turning into a Buckle Bunny, are you?"

"A what?"

"Buckle Bunny. The girls with sparkly belt buckles and too much makeup."

"What's the point of makeup out here? It would melt off straight away." She shrugged and readjusted the hat, wondering briefly where he had found it.

Darcy led his mount out of the paddock, leaning from his seat to open the gate and again to close it after Molly had walked through.

"You look like you know what you're doing," he said, reclaiming her attention.

"It's all coming back to me now." She reached down and stroked Molly's warm neck fondly. "So where are we going?"

"We need to track the bore lines and make sure water can flow through for the cows."

"What's a bore line?"

"It's over here." He pointed toward a tree line where a shallow trench was filled with murky water. Cows grazed lazily nearby; one skinny cream heifer drank from the water.

Four kangaroos jumped out from the trees and scattered into the fields. "Did you see that?" she asked excitedly.

"There are heaps of roos out here. They can survive the worst drought no problem. You'll probably see emus and wild pigs along here too."

"I saw the pigs in the pen this morning." Meghan absently swatted a fly buzzing around her head.

"Wild sows. I caught them a few months ago. You can't eat wild pigs straight away, though, they have all sorts of worms. We have to feed them scraps for a few months before slaughtering. Mum wants them for Christmas."

"Do you hunt pigs regularly then?"

"If I know there's one around, especially if it's attacking the cattle, then I'll hunt it. We trap them occasionally for meat."

Meghan raised her eyebrows. "That's very self-sufficient."

"We butcher our own beef too. Used to run merino sheep when Noah was here. Dad got rid of them when Noah left, though. Shame really, I do miss lamb chops in spring. They're too expensive to buy these days."

Lulled into a dreamy state by the swaying rhythm of Molly's gait, Meghan kept her eyes on Darcy's broad back as he rode ahead. His muscles rippled as he rode along the dirt track and over a cattle grid. He turned around in the saddle suddenly, as though he could feel her eyes studying him. She looked away quickly, feeling a warm blush on her cheeks.

She battled for something to say. "What are the animals eating? Since there's hardly any grass."

"Cottonseed. It's full of enough nutrients to keep them alive, but unfortunately, it doesn't fatten them up." He pointed out a large trailer in the middle of the field. "That's our cottonseed feeder. We only have to fill it up once a month or so and they eat out of it. Occasionally, we put out some molasses lick too. They have fun eating that sticky stuff," he said with a grin.

Molly strained against the bridle as they approached a large empty paddock.

"You can let her run if you want." Darcy gestured ahead.

Meghan grinned and with a little kick Molly started to trot. With a little more encouragement, she sped up. Meghan revelled in the wind rushing past her. She glanced back to see Darcy's mount was also galloping and he was catching up. "Come on, girl," she urged Molly along.

Despite having a faster and younger mount, he stayed a meter or two behind her as they galloped across the flat field. At last, she could sense the horse tyre, so she reigned her in. Darcy pulled up beside her, slightly breathless.

"Enjoy that?" He met her gaze with a smile so warm and engaging that she tingled all over.

"That was exhilarating!" Meghan flung her head back and her hands wide.

"Once you know the lay of the land, you'll be able to take her out." Admiration glimmered in his eyes.

"That would be great. I'd like to help out as much as I can."

Heat waves shimmered around the vast nothingness before them. It was as though they were the only things foolish enough to brave the afternoon sun.

While they inspected the land, Darcy told her about the station, about his family and the history. For three generations, the McGuire family had lived and died on Brigadier Station, working through the tough times of floods, droughts and economic hardships.

"It was my great-grandfather who first settled here. He was a brigadier in World War One, he came here afterwards. People would refer to this place as the Brigadier's station. The name stuck. He became one of the most successful cattlemen of his generation." The fondness and gratitude softened his voice. "Brigadier Station is a testament to his pioneering spirit."

The long-forgotten methane smell of cattle greeted her at the same time Darcy pointed out a mob of cattle grazing hungrily. "Here are some of our weaners. We've only got about four hundred left here. The rest are on agistment."

Meghan noted their golden honey colour. "What breed are they?"

"Droughtmaster. That's a cross between Brahman

and Shorthorn. They're the best suited up here and fetch decent prices when we ship them. We also run a breeding program."

"How big is Brigadier?"

"Sixty thousand acres. We're only going to cover a small portion today."

Meghan was impressed by the vastness. Lachie had hinted that it was big, but she had had no idea of the vast size. She gazed over the flat dry plains. The boundaries of her little world so extended, further than her eyes could see.

Suddenly Molly shied and reared up, snorting in alarm. Instinctively, Meghan squeezed her thighs and held on tightly. Darcy swung from his horse and quickly caught Molly's reigns, murmuring softly and stroking her reassuringly.

"Hey, are you alright?"

Her cheeks warmed as his gaze did a quick but thorough inspection. Worry lingered in his eyes.

"I'm fine. How's Molly?" She leaned forward in the saddle and stroked Molly's neck.

"She's okay. Must have smelt a snake." He looked to a clump of stubborn brush. "That's their likely hiding spot."

Fear shimmied down her back. "Snakes?"

"Don't worry, I won't let anything happen to you."

Darcy caught her gaze and, mesmerized by those piercing blue eyes, the fear was replaced by a warm heat. Her heart beat faster. Surely it was adrenalin from the snake incident.

He was first to break the connection. "You'd better get used to it if you're going to live here. We have our fair share of danger."

$\approx$

The horses carefully picked their way across uneven terrain, sheltered by huge coolabah trees. Occasionally, Darcy pointed out birds or other things he thought might be of interest to Meghan.

Beneath her hat, her thick ponytail swung across her shoulders. She looked fragile, like a porcelain doll he had seen in a shop once. But, out here she became another part of the environment, as at home on these plains as the rabbits and kangaroos.

He stared at the view and lost himself in the desolation that stretched ahead of him. It was so damn hot. Too hot for this time of year. It had to cool down. It had to rain. Sometime.

"You were surprised when Lachie announced our engagement." Meghan's voice was etched with worry.

Darcy thought for a moment, careful not to say anything offensive, but wanting to be honest. "I'm surprised any woman could get Lachie to commit."

She laughed. "You're kidding? It wasn't really that hard."

He recalled all-nighters at the pub watching out for

his intoxicated brother who was usually found slobbering over the latest backpacker turned waitress.

"Lachie's always been a player. Or at least, he was. You've changed him. It's been so gradual I barely noticed."

"He was never like that around me. He's always been very committed."

Darcy arched his eyebrows in surprise. "How long have you two been together?"

"Eight months."

"That's a pretty quick engagement then. Especially since this is your first time here. Unless he's planning on moving to Townsville?" He couldn't imagine Lachie giving up his birthright.

"No, we'll live here on the station."

"How do you know you'll like it?"

"I just do." She shrugged. "I don't mind cities and Townsville only has 170,000 people so it's not really that big. Just large enough for good shopping, pubs, and live entertainment, but small enough to find a quiet space when the crowds get too much."

She turned her attention to the never-ending horizon. "But, when I see these dusty fields and gum trees it's like I'm coming home. I guess that doesn't make sense. But it's true."

Darcy knew that feeling well. Whenever he returned from a trip, he felt relieved, like he could breathe again. The dust was his oxygen; he needed it to survive.

"Country life is tough. We all work hard, even Mum. A tree change doesn't mean life slows down."

"I can see that."

He pushed back his hat and scowled at the land. "Some fellas get sick of looking at the same view every day. Being isolated on a station in the thick of a blazing summer can drive people crazy. It's not an easy life if you're not used to it."

The wistful expression on her face made him realise how long it had been since he'd had a conversation with a woman who wasn't related to him or someone else's wife. He really needed to get out more.

"I don't think I could ever get sick of this place." Her words were soft. He wondered if she realised she'd spoken aloud. For a smart woman, she seemed caught up in the romance of the outback. He hoped, for her sake and Lachie's, she was prepared for a hard slog. Especially if the drought went on much longer.

Darcy knew of city girls who moved to the area hoping to meet a wealthy, handsome station heir. Mostly they returned home disheartened. Sometimes leaving broken marriages in their wake. But Meghan seemed honest in her intentions.

Cockatoos squawked above them as he took the lead as the path narrowed and the homestead came into sight. He contemplated the future and what having Meghan living with them would mean. He would have a sister-in-law. Another person to help out around the house and the station. A reminder that he would never have a wife and a family of his own unless he put himself back out there. He sighed. He couldn't risk another heartbreak. Meghan might think she was tough enough. He hoped she proved that to be true. But she would be one in a million. He wasn't as lucky as his brother.

Meghan's beautiful face would remind him of that every day.

To continue reading go to: www.books2read.com/TheBrothersofBrigadierStation

ACKNOWLEDGMENTS

My sincere thanks to my editor and mentor Annie Seaton, who has again done wonders with her advice and is such an inspiration to other authors.

To my best-buddy and talented writer friend Kelly Ethan and my step mother Lynda - thank you for believing in me and this story. Also to Renee Clasie for her help and advice. Scotty was inspired by her amazing son Connor. Keep up the great work!

A big thank you and much love to my family for all your support and for putting up with me while I write. I love you all.

And to you, dear reader, thank you for choosing this book to read. I know there are many other distractions and entertainment options available these days, so thank you for joining Paige, Logan and me on this journey.

ABOUT THE AUTHOR

Sarah Williams spent her childhood chasing sheep, riding horses and picking Kiwi fruit on the family orchard in rural New Zealand. After a decade travelling, Sarah moved to North Queensland to enjoy the warm weather and to work with Crocodiles.

When she's not absorbed in her fictional writing world, Sarah is running after her family of four kids, one husband, two dogs and a cat. She loves to help her peers achieve their publishing dreams.

Sarah is regularly checking social media when she really should be cleaning.

To receive updates and free books, sign up for her mailing list.

www.facebook.com/sarahwilliamswriter
www.twitter.com/SarahW_Writer
www.sarahwilliamsauthor.com

You can find her online at:
www.sarahwilliamsauthor.com